PRAISE FOR *THE QUICK GUIDE TO SIMULTANEOUS, HYBRID, AND BLENDED LEARNING*

If you want to work smarter versus harder in this time of distance learning, this book is for you! Schools and teachers worldwide face unique challenges as they work to accommodate and transform the methods in which they provide quality learning and teaching through various formats of distance learning. *The Quick Guide to Simultaneous, Hybrid, and Blended Learning* provides the needed clarity and specificity in how to navigate developing and managing quality teaching and learning experiences in any distance learning environment or platform. Douglas Fisher, Nancy Frey, John Almarode, and Aleigha Henderson-Rosser offer practical and authentic ideas on how to maximize and adapt for student learning and engagement in an ever-changing environment. The timing of this book is impeccable and will transform the ways in which schools and teachers intentionally plan and deliver quality instructional practices.

Debra Cale
Elementary Principal
Dallas Center-Grimes CSD
Dallas Center, IA

As an educator in a large urban district that utilizes all three of these models to help us deliver on our promise of equity, I can honestly say that *The Quick Guide to Simultaneous, Hybrid, and Blended Learning* offers every educator the entry point they need to increase students' learning, collaboration, and agency in any context. Through multiple research-based, classroom-tested practices and examples, this book gives educators the practical strategies and structures we need to enhance our simultaneous instruction. A must-read, *The Quick Guide* confronts the doubts and challenges associated with simultaneous and hybrid environments by offering implement-right-away solutions that inspire readers to see that, regardless of the modality or context in which students learn, learning at high levels is still possible for all students.

Kierstan Barbee
Assessment for Learning Coordinator
Dallas, TX

This is the book that I have been waiting for! After schools shut down because of the pandemic and we realized that our return to school would not be "business as usual," I was having a difficult time imagining what school would look like in a simultaneous learning environment. This guide gives me permission to use what I know but extends the paradigm in which I was thinking. Clarity, a crucial component in designing effective learning experiences, is addressed and amplified in this guide to help allay some of my concerns. Student engagement, something at the forefront of every educator's mind, is also on the minds of the authors. This guidebook is easy to follow but allows the reader to take the ideas and adapt them to their own situation. So helpful!

Melanie Janzen
Curriculum Coordinator, Secondary Mathematics
San Bernardino County Superintendent of Schools
San Bernardino, CA

This book is a multipurpose tool for the educator's toolbox. The information and examples combine for methodologies to not only be used during a pandemic but to truly provide a bridge into future learning and instruction.

Douglas Howell
Superintendent
Pocatello-Chubbuck School District
Pocatello, ID

The Quick Guide to Simultaneous, Hybrid, and Blended Learning by Douglas Fisher, Nancy Frey, John Almarode, and Aleigha Henderson-Rosser is a practical guide for educators at all levels. From definitions to learning models to digital tools, this book has a little bit of everything for educators who are implementing remote learning (and aren't we all?)! The potential learning models described are especially helpful for academic administrators determining how to pivot to remote learning, and weekly plans for each learning type support classroom implementation. The authors also provide practical solutions for common problems in remote learning, including student engagement and how to teach in-person and remote students simultaneously. I'll be flipping through my *Quick Guide* to apply these solutions for semesters to come.

Elizabeth E. Smith
Assistant Professor of Education
Vice Provost for Academic Initiatives and Faculty Affairs
The University of Tulsa, OK

This is a must-have for all involved with thinking about and involved with distance learning. This book is insightful and provides administrators and teachers with the tools and questions to think about when planning high-quality, rigorous, and engaging lessons—whether they are doing so asynchronously or synchronously. Examples and key insights from educators already immersed in the field provide yet another handy resource from which teachers and administrators can easily flip through and glean ideas. As distance learning is now changing the way in which we teach and the structure in how our students learn, this book is essential for anyone who is thinking about designing a high-quality distance learning model.

Lisa C. Chen
Director of Virtual Learning
Louisa County Public Schools
Mineral, VA

Managing technology has been a challenge for our teachers and students. *The Quick Guide to Simultaneous, Hybrid, and Blended Learning* gives teachers the techniques to deal with technical complexities in smart and creative ways. We need to save time for meaningful instruction and one of the ways we can do that is not to narrate all that we're doing to students. Give students the time to read the instructions, charts, and other visual aids, and let them take ownership of the learning process. Students are loving that autonomy!

Elizabeth Cardenas-Lopez
Director of Literacy
Evanston/Skokie School District 65
Evanston, IL

The QUICK GUIDE to

SIMULTANEOUS, HYBRID, & BLENDED LEARNING

DOUGLAS FISHER
NANCY FREY
JOHN ALMARODE
ALEIGHA HENDERSON-ROSSER

CORWIN

Fisher & Frey

FOR INFORMATION:

Corwin

A SAGE Company

2455 Teller Road

Thousand Oaks, California 91320

(800) 233-9936

www.corwin.com

SAGE Publications Ltd.

1 Oliver's Yard

55 City Road

London EC1Y 1SP

United Kingdom

SAGE Publications India Pvt. Ltd.

B 1/I 1 Mohan Cooperative Industrial Area

Mathura Road, New Delhi 110 044

India

SAGE Publications Asia-Pacific Pte. Ltd.

18 Cross Street #10-10/11/12

China Square Central

Singapore 048423

Cover illustration by Taryl Hansen

Printed in the United States of America

ISBN 978-1-0718-5165-4

Library of Congress Control Number: 2021903644

Director and Publisher, Corwin Classroom: Lisa Luedeke

Content Development Editor: Jessica Vidal

Editorial Assistant: Caroline Timmings

Production Editor: Melanie Birdsall

Copy Editor: Diane DiMura

Typesetter: C&M Digitals (P) Ltd.

Proofreader: Theresa Kay

Indexer: Sheila Hill

Cover Designer: Gail Buschman

Marketing Manager: Deena Meyer

This book is printed on acid-free paper.

21 22 23 24 25 10 9 8 7 6 5 4 3 2 1

Contents

Introduction

The boundaries of teaching and learning in the preK–12 classrooms have been expanded, stretched, and blurred as we develop different approaches and pathways for reaching and teaching students. Designing and implementing rigorous and engaging experiences that move learning forward has always been, and will continue to be, the impetus behind what we do in our schools and classrooms. What has changed, and continues to change, is the context in which these experiences occur. For many of us, calculus moved to the couch, language arts to the living room, and physical education to the patio. Distance learning was the new normal.

Distance learning is what prompted the sudden expanding, stretching, and blurring of the boundary between home, classroom, and school. Distance learning has existed for a while in some contexts within education. Perhaps you remember when your teacher rolled the television into the classroom, and you watched current events in real time, such as a space shuttle launch or the 9/11 terrorist attacks. Or you may remember a science teacher flipping through your catalog of laserdiscs to display the perfect interactive visual of a beating heart to your students. Or perhaps you can remember a time when an expert "visited" your classroom via teleconferencing to lend their expertise to a lecture. Did you know that Chicago schools educated over 315,000 students for several weeks in 1937 via the radio due to the polio outbreak? Students tuned into different stations based on their grade level and there was a call center staffed by teachers to provide additional help. These various contexts have used some form of technology innovation, a departure from face-to-face instruction in which students received information from the teacher alone and engaged students in a different medium of receiving instruction.

But that changed as a result of COVID. As parents, guardians, and primary childcare providers, we found ourselves in the car loop picking up laptops, hotspots, books, and school meals. As teachers, we found ourselves attending ongoing professional learning, researching and leveraging available instructional technology to ensure continuity of learning, supporting our learners in finding, gathering, creating, and sharing information (see Figure I.1).

Finally, instructional leaders tackled the challenge of liaising between teachers and families to ensure learners had access to school and "logged on" to class.

While there are a variety of perspectives, there are data that suggest, by and large, we did what families, instructional leaders, teachers, and our students have done many times before. We stepped up to the challenge and made the best of the current situation (see Kuhfeld et al., 2020b). This same data points us in the direction of opportunities for growth and improvement. And that should be expected in any teaching and learning environment. After all, continuous improvement is the hallmark of expertise in teaching (Rickards, Hattie, & Fields, 2021). But the point we are trying to make is that,

CONTINUOUS IMPROVEMENT IS THE HALLMARK OF EXPERTISE IN TEACHING.

1.1 FUNCTIONS AND TOOLS

Teacher wants students to	Student Engagement Opportunities	Sample Digital Resources
Find Information	• Can locate information sources • Can organize and analyze information sources for accuracy and utility to the task • Locating information is driven by curiosity and topic	• Wakelet • Google/Google Scholar • Quizlet • Pear Deck • eBooks
Use Information	• Can cite sources of information • Makes judgments about how best to use information • Asks questions the information provokes	• Evernote • OneNote • Flipgrid • Grammarly • PlayPosit • TurnItIn • Nearpod • Didax Math Manipulatives • Toytheater Virtual Manipulatives • Boomwriter
Create Information	• Can write and discuss information according to grade-level expectations • Transforms information in order to explore ideas new to the learner • Takes academic risks to innovate	• GSuite for Education • Office 365 • ThingLink • iMovie • Padlet • Seesaw • Screencastify • Google Drawings • Jamboard • StoryboardThat
Share Information	• Accurately matches purpose to the audience • Uses metacognitive thinking to identify the best strategies for the stated purpose • Is resourceful and resilient	• Animoto • Storybird • WeVideo • Jamboard • YouTube

Source: Adapted from Fisher, D., Frey, N., & Hattie, J. (2020). *The distance learning playbook, grades K–12: Teaching for engagement and impact in any setting*. Corwin.

while stressful, teachers and learners demonstrated that distance learning was possible. In fact, there are aspects of distance learning that we will bring back to face-to-face learning environments as lessons learned. The 21st century teaching and learning practices that teachers have adopted have elevated the conversation around integrating technology in the teaching and learning cycle. These lessons learned will pave the way for us to come back better.

But hold on a second. Here we go again! Teaching and learning exclusively on Zoom, Google Meets, or WebEx is one thing. Similarly, learners engaged in face-to-face learning in a socially distanced school and classroom, closer to what we are all comfortable and familiar with, have advantages and disadvantages. But teaching and learning in a school or classroom where some learners are "logged on" at the same time as some learners are face-to-face is yet another expanding, stretching, and blurring of the boundaries. In Atlanta, Georgia, this is referred to as *Roomies and Zoomies*. This *simultaneous learning environment* requires an entirely different conversation. And that is exactly the conversation we aim to have over the next six chapters—simultaneously teaching *Roomies and Zoomies*. Of course, there are other platforms that school systems use, but for ease of discussion, we will refer to Roomies and Zoomies to distinguish the various learning situations. Throughout this book, we use the evidence from Visible Learning® (www.visiblelearningmetax.com) to make our recommendations. We recognize that the vast majority of studies in this database were not conducted during distance learning (but some were), but we believe that the implications from the evidence are still important. In this database, the average effect size is 0.40. Thus anything over 0.40 is an above-average effect and should ensure that students are learning.

IN ATLANTA, GEORGIA, THIS IS REFERRED TO AS ROOMIES AND ZOOMIES.

TERMINOLOGY

Before we go any further into this conversation, we want to make sure we are clear on the terminology of what is often referred to as the grammar of schooling (Cuban, 1993). One of the outcomes or side effects of this expanded view of teaching and learning is the potential for us to get lost in the lingo. Let's begin with distance learning.

Distance learning. We use the term *distance learning* to refer to the broader context of teaching and learning through an online platform. Teachers and students engaged in distance learning are doing so completely through the use of Zoom, Google Meets, Microsoft Teams, WebEx, SeeSaw, Canvas, and Blackboard, for example. Neither the teacher nor the student needs to physically be in a school or on a campus. Within distance learning, however, is the option for synchronous and asynchronous learning. We use distance learning to describe situations in which students are learning remotely from the school building.

Synchronous learning. If teachers and students are engaged in teaching and learning in real time or live, they are learning synchronously. Synchronous learning involves a class or daily schedule that requires individuals to log on at a specific time for a predetermined duration. In Figure I.2, daily Zoom sessions are scheduled for 8:30 a.m. and 12:30 p.m. You may think synchronous learning includes face-to-face instruction. After all, learners in face-to-face learning get off the school bus and walk into classrooms organized by class and daily schedules. The difference between these two contexts is the location. Synchronous learning does not occur in the same geographic location. Learners are at home, at the local Boys and Girls Club, or any other location.

I.2 CANVAS HOMEPAGE WITH SYNCHRONOUS AND ASYNCHRONOUS LEARNING SCHEDULE

1.0 Week 1 (Evidence for Evolution) Overview

Overview:

How do scientists know how organisms have changed over time? This week you will learn about the various lines of evidence that support evolution.

Unit Success Criteria:

☑ **Provide multiple pieces of evidence to explain common ancestry.**

☐ Describe the conditions necessary for evolution to occur via natural selection.

☐ Explain how adaptations provide an advantage in a given environment.

☐ Construct an explanation for how changes in the environment may result in speciation.

Zoom Schedule (Synchronous):	Finish by Friday (Asynchronous):
Monday ☐ 1.1 🔹 Extinction Events Article **Tuesday** ☐ 1.3 📄 Explore Your Inner Animal ☐ 1.5 🔹 Scientists Grow 'Dinosaur Legs' on a Chicken for the First Time Article **Thursday** ☐ 1.6 📄 Molecular Evidence for Evolution **Friday** ☐ 1.8 📄 Sheep Eye Dissection	☐ 1.2 🎥 When Will The Next Extinction Event Occur? Video ☐ 1.4 🎥 B-Rex Video Discussion Board ☐ 1.7 🎥 The Science of Skin Color PlayPosit ☐ 🔵 Science Weekly #11: Evidence for Evolution ☐ ⬛ Empowers- Week 1

Source: Courtesy of Kim Elliot. Image source: Cloud: Bigtunaonline/iStock.com

Asynchronous learning. Much like synchronous learning, asynchronous learning can occur in any geographic location. However, in an asynchronous environment, teachers provide a learning progression and the necessary resources for students to engage in the learning at their own pace and time. While there are time limits and due dates on this progression (i.e., one week to complete the tasks or "by the end of the day"), students are responsible for managing their own time and pace within the time limits and before the due dates. You will notice in Figure I.2 that there are tasks on the daily agenda that are asynchronous.

Face-to-face learning. This concept is well-known and reflects what we are most familiar with in preK–12 schools and classrooms. For the purposes of our conversation about

Roomies and Zoomies, we mean face-to-face learning to be when students and teachers meet at the same time in the same place, even if socially distanced.

Blended learning. The name says it all. In blended learning, students are engaged in both distance learning and face-to-face learning, but not at the same time. For example, learners may engage in distance learning for a particular course or during a day of the week and then in a face-to-face learning environment for other courses or on other days. When we discuss blended learning in this book, we are referring to this particular learning context. The idea of blended learning existed prior to the pandemic and was generally understood to mean that students had some control over the time, place, path, or pace of their learning. In this traditional model of blended learning, students use technology as a tool to help drive their own learning. But it was rare to have students learning at home during the day in a blended learning situation.

Hybrid learning. This term has been used to describe any number of different formats of school, and there is a lack of consensus about what this term really means. Generally speaking, hybrid learning is used to describe situations in which students learn part-time with a teacher in a physical school classroom and part-time online. Many students, pre-pandemic, experienced hybrid learning within the classroom as software programs delivered some of the learning experiences. By definition, hybrid learning does not require any remote learning time. And students may not have control over the time, place, path, or pace of their learning. Thus, we have adopted the term *simultaneous* learning to describe new ways to organize the learning experiences for students.

In some instances, school districts use hybrid and blended interchangeably. And many districts have introduced the term *remote learning* to identify when a student is learning in a setting other than the school.

Simultaneous learning. We define *simultaneous learning* as the combining of teaching some learners at a distance and others face-to-face learning in the same learning experience. As we mentioned previously, and you have likely experienced, simultaneous learning requires an entirely different conversation around the planning, developing, and implementing of rigorous and engaging experiences that move learning forward. Let's look at a few examples. Ms. Lewanowicz, a third-grade teacher at Cherrywood Elementary School, welcomes one-half of her class into room 6, where they engage in socially distanced, face-to-face learning. At the same time, the other half of her learners are logged on to Zoom and projected on the interactive whiteboard.

Sometimes in simultaneous learning, the Roomies can see the Zoomies, but the Zoomies can't see the Roomies. In other cases, the teacher can see the Roomies and Zoomies and each group of students can also see each other. The Roomies are logged into their computer with the Zoomies (on the same Zoom session). Or the teacher can use the document camera and point it at the room to show a classroom view. The teacher can then engage with both groups of students at the same time. This allows the teacher to foster community among the two groups and eases the amount of preparation that a teacher may have to do to meet the needs of both groups separately.

At Sunset Valley High School, Ms. Marquez starts each day with a shortened schedule where she meets with all of her U.S. government classes on Zoom. Learners at Sunset Valley High School attend all four of the classes for approximately 30 minutes each, as Zoomies. In the afternoon, half of her U.S. government students come to school as

Roomies, while the other half engages in asynchronous, distance learning. Tomorrow, they will switch places. In this model, the Roomies do not have the opportunity to interact with the Zoomies. For both Ms. Lewanowicz and Ms. Marquez, they must think about their approaches to teaching and learning in a different way—blending together their thinking about face-to-face learning with their thinking about learning at a distance. The next page provides examples of reflective questions that Ms. Lewanowicz and Ms. Marquez use to guide their thinking and decisions about designing and implementing rigorous and engaging experiences in a simultaneous learning environment.

In reality, there is a continuum in terms of time and learning (see Figure I.3) for asynchronous and synchronous learning.

I.3   ASYNCHRONOUS AND SYNCHRONOUS TIME AND LEARNING CONTINUUM

Time Continuum

Asynchronous Time ———————— Synchronous Time

Students work on their own pace on tasks that allow them to preview and review content as well as practice and apply what has been taught.

The teacher and students are together online or in person to enable communication, collaboration, and critical discussion. Because they are together, the teacher can provide timely and appropriate support that may include but is not limited to redirection, clarification, scaffolding, and differentiation.

Learning Continuum

Asynchronous Learning ———————— Synchronous Learning

Students take ownership of their learning by monitoring their progress toward achieving the Success Criteria. The teacher engineers high-quality learning experiences that are purposefully aligned with the Success Criteria. As a result, students are engaged learners who take on the role of problem solver.

The teacher and students are interacting at the same time, place, and pace in an engaging and collaborative way. The teacher frequently checks for understanding to provide feedback individually or to the whole class. Teachers prioritize and enable connection, discussion, and interaction.

Source: Fontana Unified School District Elementary Instruction Team (2020).

Reflective Questions for Teaching Roomies and Zoomies

- What are my students learning?

- Why are they learning this?

- What does success look like?

- What approaches or strategies will I use to engage face-to-face learners *simultaneously* with my distance learners?

- How will I foster community between both sets of students?

- What aspects of the learning are best suited for asynchronous learning?

- What aspects of the learning are best suited for synchronous learning?

- How will I scaffold teaching and learning to ensure learners are appropriately challenged?

- How will I encourage feedback from my distance learners?

- Finally, how will I monitor student learning in my face-to-face learners *simultaneously* with my distance learners?

We will take a close look at each of these questions in the chapters that follow. Teaching and learning in the simultaneous learning environment does not require that we reinvent the wheel or throw everything out and start over. Instead, we must work collaboratively with our PLCs, instructional technology department, instructional leadership teams, content-area colleagues, or grade-level planning teams to combine what has worked in both face-to-face and distance learning environments. After all, the definition of *simultaneous learning* uses the term *combine*. Let's combine the best parts of both as we continue to move learning forward. Again, this may be stressful at the start, but possible. Let's start by looking at the different models of simultaneous learning. One of these models may match the particular approach in your district or school, while some of you may find this list helpful in deciding the particular approach you might take in the near future.

DIFFERENT MODELS OF SIMULTANEOUS LEARNING

There are many different models of simultaneous learning, each of which reflects adaptions based on the local context of the district or school. A one-size-fits-all approach does not necessarily accommodate the needs of the students or teachers or may not be realistic given the challenges associated with transportation, technology, materials, and supplies. While describing every possible permutation of face-to-face and distance learning for implementing simultaneous learning would be impossible, we wanted to look at three specific models that are most common.

A-B Model

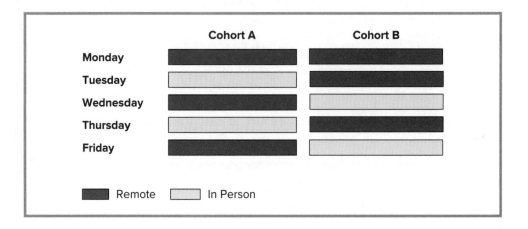

Let's return to Ms. Lewanowicz, the third-grade teacher from Cherrywood Elementary School. Her school has implemented the A–B model for simultaneous learning. On Monday, all learners are engaged in asynchronous, distance learning. Learners are provided a learning progression and the necessary resources through the school division's learning management system, Canvas. These tasks include a variety of review tasks from the previous week or experiences that are designed to activate and identify prior or background knowledge. The specific details of these tasks will be further explored in subsequent chapters. For the purposes of understanding the A–B model, this day is set aside for asynchronous learning while all teachers, including Ms. Lewanowicz and her third-grade team, engage in planning, professional learning, and essential meetings (e.g., Individualized Education Plans or IEP meetings and parent–teacher conferences).

For the remainder of the week, learners are divided into two different groups based on which of the remaining two days of the week they are face-to-face and which two days they are learning at a distance (see Figure I.4). For example, some students attend face-to-face on Tuesdays and Thursdays (the A Group) while other students attend face-to-face on Wednesdays and Fridays (the B Group). What makes this particular model a simultaneous learning model is that when the A Group is engaged in face-to-face learning, the B Group is engaged in synchronous and asynchronous distance learning. As you may recall, Ms. Lewanowicz projects her Zoomies on the interactive whiteboard so that her Roomies can see their peers.

I.4 THE A–B MODEL FOR SIMULTANEOUS LEARNING

	Monday	Tuesday	Wednesday	Thursday	Friday
A Group	Asynchronous, distance learning	Face-to-face learning	Synchronous and asynchronous, distance learning	Face-to-face learning	Synchronous and asynchronous, distance learning
B Group	Asynchronous, distance learning	Synchronous and asynchronous, distance learning	Face-to-face learning	Synchronous and asynchronous, distance learning	Face-to-face learning

For the A–B model, Ms. Lewanowicz and her colleagues at Cherrywood Elementary School are moving between

➡ Asynchronous, distance learning

➡ Face-to-face learning combined with synchronous learning

➡ Face-to-face learning combined with asynchronous learning

Those last two approaches are what make this model a simultaneous learning model. While we highlighted this model in an elementary classroom, this model has also been implemented in both middle schools and high schools.

Split Day Model

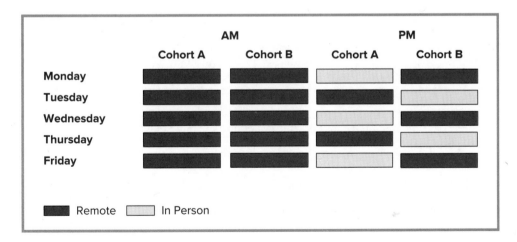

Now recall the high school U.S. government teacher, Ms. Marquez. The split day model for simultaneous learning splits the day in half, along with which group of students are learning at a distance and which group of students are engaged in synchronous learning. Sunset Valley High School uses a 4 × 4 block. For the faculty at Sunset Valley High School, every day starts with synchronous distance learning for all learners. Instead of the traditional 90-minute blocks, learners log on to Google Meets for 30 minutes for each class. The day and week are then split. For example, on Monday, half of the students transition to face-to-face learning for the remainder of the school day. The other half of the students participate in asynchronous learning.

On Tuesday, the day begins just as it did on Monday with shortened 4 × 4 block synchronous learning sessions on Google Meets for all learners. However, on Tuesday, the group of learners who previously engaged in asynchronous learning spends the afternoon in face-to-face learning. Those who were face-to-face on Monday engage in asynchronous, distance learning. This is an example of what some school districts may refer to as hybrid learning. The students are learning in two different learning environments (see Figure I.5).

I.5 THE SPLIT DAY FOR SIMULTANEOUS LEARNING

	Monday	Tuesday	Wednesday	Thursday	Friday
AM	All learners engaged in synchronous, distance learning	All learners engaged in synchronous, distance learning	All learners engaged in synchronous, distance learning	All learners engaged in synchronous, distance learning	All learners engaged in synchronous, distance learning
PM	Half of the learners in face-to-face learning Half of the learners in asynchronous, distance learning	Half of the learners in face-to-face learning Half of the learners in asynchronous, distance learning	Half of the learners in face-to-face learning Half of the learners in asynchronous, distance learning	Half of the learners in face-to-face learning Half of the learners in asynchronous, distance learning	Half of the learners in face-to-face learning Half of the learners in asynchronous, distance learning

For the split day, Ms. Marquez and her colleagues at Sunset Valley High School are moving between

➡ Synchronous, distance learning

➡ Face-to-face learning combined with asynchronous learning

The learning that occurs in the afternoon of each day is what makes this model a simultaneous learning model. While we highlighted this model in a 4 × 4 block high school, this model has been implemented in elementary schools, middle schools, and high schools that operate using different scheduling models. We will look more at the planning and implementation of these learning experiences soon.

Full Week Model

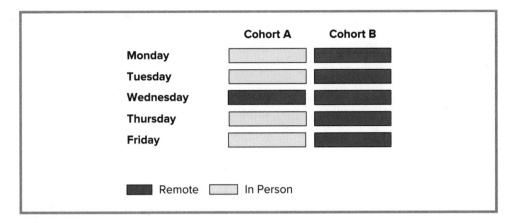

The final model we want to highlight usually develops as a result of the school division or district providing a choice to their learners and their families. For example, Sanchez Independent School District (ISD) surveyed all of their families, asking if they preferred that their child or children attended school face-to-face or if they preferred to engage in distance learning. Based on the responses and their ability to accommodate each family's preferences, learners that wished to physically come to school were allowed to do so four days out of the week. Those learners who requested to take part in learning from a distance were allowed to do so as well. Given that this particular model involves simultaneous learning each day of the week, Sanchez ISD decided to make Wednesday an asynchronous, distance learning day (see Figure I.6). Much like the A–B model, Wednesday was set aside for teachers to engage in planning, professional learning, and essential meetings (e.g., Individualized Education Plans or IEP meetings and parent–teacher conferences).

I.6 THE FULL WEEK MODEL FOR SIMULTANEOUS LEARNING

	Monday	Tuesday	Wednesday	Thursday	Friday
Face-to-Face Group	Face-to-face learning	Face-to-face learning	Asynchronous, distance learning	Face-to-face learning	Face-to-face learning
Distance Learning Group	Synchronous and asynchronous, distance learning	Synchronous and asynchronous, distance learning	Asynchronous, distance learning	Synchronous and asynchronous, distance learning	Synchronous and asynchronous, distance learning

For the full week model, teachers and students engage in

➡ Asynchronous, distance learning

➡ Face-to-face learning combined with synchronous learning

➡ Face-to-face learning combined with asynchronous learning

As with the previous two models, the full week model works at any grade level.

LET'S NOT DOUBLE THE WORK

WHEN FOSTERING AND SUSTAINING ACTIVE STUDENT ENGAGEMENT, WE SHOULD NOT TREAT DISTANCE AND FACE-TO-FACE LEARNERS AS MUTUALLY EXCLUSIVE GROUPS.

Simultaneous learning is the combination of distance learning and face-to-face learning in the same learning experience. Unfortunately, this has led to the belief, and often the practice, of doubling the workloads of families, instructional leaders, teachers, and our students. Combining two approaches to teaching and learning must not result in an additive approach to designing and implementing rigorous and engaging experiences that move learning forward. Trying to teach two different sets of students is both stressful and unsustainable. As we have continued to emphasize, simultaneous learning requires an entirely different conversation. For example, the conversation around clarity and planning should not be about planning twice—once for distance learning and once for face-to-face. Likewise, when fostering and sustaining active student engagement, we should not treat distance and face-to-face learners as mutually exclusive groups. And finally, how we monitor student learning should reflect both contexts. Simultaneously teaching Roomies *and* Zoomies may be stressful, but it is possible when we also extract and then implement what works best from both distance learning and face-to-face learning environments. Then, and only then, can Ms. Lewanowicz, Ms. Marquez, and the teachers in Sanchez ISD find this approach possible, if stressful.

Now, let's look closer at clarity and planning for simultaneous learning. The intentional, deliberate, and purposeful planning in simultaneous learning ensures we maximize teaching and learning in the combined teaching of some learners at a distance and others face-to-face learning during the same learning experience.

1 CLARITY AND PLANNING FOR SIMULTANEOUS LEARNING

In this section:

- ☐ PLANNING FOR CLARITY IN SIMULTANEOUS LEARNING
  - WHAT ARE WE LEARNING?
  - WHY ARE WE LEARNING THIS?
  - WHAT DOES SUCCESS LOOK LIKE?

Clarity is comprised of two very important components. First, clarity about learning refers to our overall awareness of what the learning is for that day or class period; why this particular content, set of skills, and understandings are relevant; and what successful learning looks like by the end of the day or class period. The second component of clarity is ensuring that our learners have the same awareness about their learning. This definition of clarity applies to any environment, face-to-face, blended, hybrid, or distance learning, where both we and our learners must be able to answer the following questions:

➡ What are we learning?

➡ Why are we learning this?

➡ What does success look like?

Clear answers to these three questions can potentially double the rate of learning in our students (www.visiblelearningmetax.com). These answers are developed and communicated through our learning intentions, task design, and success criteria.

CLEAR ANSWERS TO THESE THREE QUESTIONS CAN POTENTIALLY DOUBLE THE RATE OF LEARNING IN OUR STUDENTS (www.VISIBLELEARNINGMETAX.COM).

- **What are we learning?** is developed and communicated through our learning intentions.

- **Why are we learning this?** is conveyed through task design and conversations with students.

- **What does success look like?** is represented by the success criteria.

Figures 1.1 and 1.2 are examples of communicating clarity through learning intentions and success criteria and ensuring an explicit connection to why this learning is important. These two examples are presented through an online learning platform at the same time they can be presented to face-to-face learners. This is what makes clarity in simultaneous learning a bit different from clarity in other learning environments.

In simultaneous learning, we do not have the benefit of proximity with our synchronous and asynchronous distance learners. For example, Ms. Lewanowicz, Ms. Marquez, and the teachers in Sanchez ISD can easily walk up to or respond to questions from their face-to-face learners, or Roomies. They can support and maintain clarity on the spot. However, their Zoomies, while working toward the same learning and outcomes, are not within reach and may not be immediately accessible during simultaneous teaching and learning. Assessing whether or not learners are clear about their learning presents the same challenge. Therefore, we have to not only establish clarity around the *what*, *why*, and *how* of the day's learning, we have to ensure that there are scaffolds in place for those learners not physically with us in the classroom.

Clarity for learning is not a new concept. Initially introduced by Rosenshine and Furst (1971), clarity is now accompanied by a growing body of evidence that shows clarity for learning has a significant influence on teaching and learning (e.g., Cruikshank, 1985; Saphier, Haley-Speca, & Gower, 2008; Simonds, 1997). What is new to the conversation is the establishing and maintaining of clarity in simultaneous learning. As we mentioned in the introduction, this does not mean that we are doubling our workload by

EXAMPLES OF LEARNING INTENTIONS AND SUCCESS CRITERIA

SUCCESS CRITERIA!

This Week's Learning Targets/ Intentions	Tasks/Assessments	Success Criteria	Before Rating	After Rating
I am learning about • **How waves travel through matter.** • **Loud and soft sounds.** • **The different types of waves (mechanical, transverse, longitudinal, sound).**	☐ Complete preassessment. ☐ Watch phenomenon video. ☐ Complete "Encounter the Phenomenon" document observations when a tuning fork is hit hard and soft. ☐ Read "At the Core of It" and complete the graphic organizer. ☐ Complete the "Strike That" lab and reflection question.	I can ☐ Predict if a ball thrown in the ocean will be pushed back to shore or not. ☐ Document observations and generate questions about loud and soft sounds. ☐ Define *mechanical wave, transverse wave, longitudinal wave,* and *sound wave.* ☐ Describe the features of *P*-waves and *S*-waves. ☐ Explain why the rice behaves differently when the glass is struck hard and soft.		

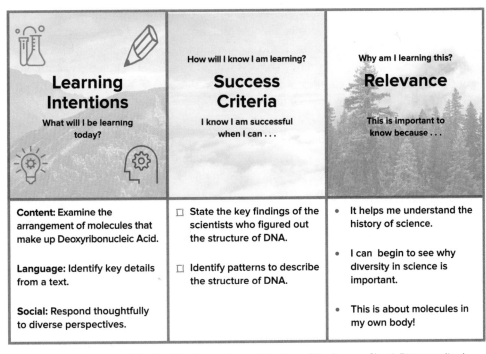

	How will I know I am learning?	Why am I learning this?
Learning Intentions What will I be learning today?	**Success Criteria** I know I am successful when I can . . .	**Relevance** This is important to know because . . .
Content: Examine the arrangement of molecules that make up Deoxyribonucleic Acid. **Language:** Identify key details from a text. **Social:** Respond thoughtfully to diverse perspectives.	☐ State the key findings of the scientists who figured out the structure of DNA. ☐ Identify patterns to describe the structure of DNA.	• It helps me understand the history of science. • I can begin to see why diversity in science is important. • This is about molecules in my own body!

Image sources: Mountain: Gilitukha/iStock.com; Icons: Enis Aksoy/iStock.com; Cloud: Bigtunaonline/iStock.com; Trees: Cassidy Jankowski/iStock.com

developing different sets of learning intentions and success criteria every day for each learning context (e.g., face-to-face, synchronous, and asynchronous). Instead, we have to differentiate the communication of clarity by providing scaffolds for different learning contexts. Zoomies may be working toward the same learning intentions and success criteria as the Roomies, but the approach will differ. The principles of clarity are the same; the translation and application into this environment are what need further discussion, beginning with the planning for clarity in simultaneous learning.

PLANNING FOR CLARITY IN SIMULTANEOUS LEARNING

Fendick (1990) defines *clarity* as the compilation of organizing instruction, explaining content, providing examples, guided practice, and assessment of learning. These specific components of clarity are rooted in the planning process and make the content and practices accessible to the learners. In simultaneous learning, our conversations during asynchronous learning days (the A–B model and the full week model) or during our planning time in the split day model should include conversations about the development of learning intentions, success criteria, and differentiating the communication of these to our learners. Task design is also an essential part of planning for clarity, but we save those conversations for later chapters.

WHAT IS NEW TO THE CONVERSATION IS THE ESTABLISHING AND MAINTAINING OF CLARITY IN SIMULTANEOUS LEARNING.

As always, planning for clarity begins with analyzing the standards and identifying the essential knowledge, skills, and understandings associated with the specific topic or content. Again, identifying the nouns or concepts, analyzing the verbs or skills, and developing learning progressions is not new. But, once we have developed our learning progressions, this is where the work of planning for simultaneous learning takes a path that is a bit different from clarity conversations in the other learning environments. In addition to answering the three questions from above, developing learning intentions and success criteria, we now have to consider where specific learning will take place (e.g., in the classroom or outside of the classroom) and how we will communicate that to our learners across those different contexts. In other words, for each of the key concepts, skills, and understandings, we have to differentiate the communicating of clarity based on the context. Figure 1.3 is a planning template that helps organize this part of the clarity and planning process.

The template in Figure 1.3 supports planning in the A–B model and includes several different aspects of simultaneous learning that will further explore in subsequent chapters. Figures 1.4 and 1.5 show what this looks like in the split day and full week models, respectively.

1.3 PLANNING TEMPLATE FOR THE A–B MODEL OF SIMULTANEOUS LEARNING

Content: _____ Grade: _____

Week of: (DATE) _____

This Week's Learning Targets/Intentions	Tasks/Assessments	Success Criteria
I am learning . . .		I can . . .

Monday—Asynchronous Day	Tuesday—Simultaneous Day	Wednesday—Simultaneous Day	Thursday—Simultaneous Day	Friday—Simultaneous Day
Groups A and B (both Asynchronous)	Group A (Face-to-Face)	Group B (Face-to-Face)	Group A (Face-to-Face)	Group B (Face-to-Face)
Attend:	Attend:	Attend:	Attend:	Attend:
Read:	Read:	Read:	Read:	Read:
Watch:	Watch:	Watch:	Watch:	Watch:

(Continued)

(Continued)

Monday—Asynchronous Day	Tuesday—Simultaneous Day	Wednesday—Simultaneous Day	Thursday—Simultaneous Day	Friday—Simultaneous Day
	Discuss:	Discuss:	Discuss:	Discuss:
	Turn in:	Turn in:	Turn in:	Turn in:
	Group B (Synchronous/ Asynchronous)	Group A (Synchronous/ Asynchronous)	Group B (Synchronous/ Asynchronous)	Group A (Synchronous/ Asynchronous)
	Attend:	Attend:	Attend:	Attend:
	Read:	Read:	Read:	Read:
	Watch:	Watch:	Watch:	Watch:
	Discuss:	Discuss:	Discuss:	Discuss:
	Turn in:	Turn in:	Turn in:	Turn in:

Source: Adapted from Fisher, D., Frey, N., & Hattie, J. (2020). *The distance learning playbook, grades K–12: Teaching for engagement and impact in any setting.* Corwin.

1.4 PLANNING TEMPLATE FOR THE SPLIT DAY MODEL OF SIMULTANEOUS LEARNING

Content: _____   Grade: _____

Week of: (DATE) _____

This Week's Learning Targets/Intentions	Tasks/Assessments	Success Criteria
I am learning . . .		I can . . .

Monday	Tuesday	Wednesday	Thursday	Friday
AM (Synchronous)	**AM (Synchronous)**	**AM (Synchronous)**	**AM (Synchronous)**	**AM (Synchronous)**
Attend:	Attend:	Attend:	Attend:	Attend:
Read:	Read:	Read:	Read:	Read:
Watch:	Watch:	Watch:	Watch:	Watch:
Discuss:	Discuss:	Discuss:	Discuss:	Discuss:
Turn in:	Turn in:	Turn in:	Turn in:	Turn in:

(Continued)

(Continued)

Monday	Tuesday	Wednesday	Thursday	Friday
PM (Face-to-Face)	**PM (Face-to-Face)**	**PM (Face-to-Face)**	**PM (Face-to-Face)**	**PM (Face-to-Face)**
Attend:	Attend:	Attend:	Attend:	Attend:
Read:	Read:	Read:	Read:	Read:
Watch:	Watch:	Watch:	Watch:	Watch:
Discuss:	Discuss:	Discuss:	Discuss:	Discuss:
Turn in:	Turn in:	Turn in:	Turn in:	Turn in:
PM (Asynchronous)	**PM (Asynchronous)**	**PM (Asynchronous)**	**PM (Asynchronous)**	**PM (Asynchronous)**
Attend:	Attend:	Attend:	Attend:	Attend:
Read:	Read:	Read:	Read:	Read:
Watch:	Watch:	Watch:	Watch:	Watch:
Discuss:	Discuss:	Discuss:	Discuss:	Discuss:
Turn in:	Turn in:	Turn in:	Turn in:	Turn in:

Source: Adapted from Fisher, D., Frey, N., & Hattie, J. (2020). *The distance learning playbook, grades K–12: Teaching for engagement and impact in any setting.* Corwin.

1.5 PLANNING TEMPLATE FOR THE FULL WEEK MODEL OF SIMULTANEOUS LEARNING

Content: _____ Grade: _____

Week of: (DATE) _____

This Week's Learning Targets/Intentions	Tasks/Assessments	Success Criteria
I am learning . . .		I can . . . .

Monday—Simultaneous Day	Tuesday—Simultaneous Day	Wednesday—Asynchronous Day	Thursday—Simultaneous Day	Friday—Simultaneous Day
Face-to-Face Group	Face-to-Face Group	(All Asynchronous)	Face-to-Face Group	Face-to-Face Group
Attend:	Attend:	Attend:	Attend:	Attend:
Read:	Read:	Read:	Read:	Read:
Watch:	Watch:	Watch:	Watch:	Watch:

(Continued)

(Continued)

Monday—Simultaneous Day	Tuesday—Simultaneous Day	Wednesday—Asynchronous Day	Thursday—Simultaneous Day	Friday—Simultaneous Day
Discuss:	Discuss:	Discuss:	Discuss:	Discuss:
Turn in:	Turn in:	Turn in:	Turn in:	Turn in:
Synchronous/ Asynchronous Group	**Synchronous/ Asynchronous Group**		**Synchronous/ Asynchronous Group**	**Synchronous/ Asynchronous Group**
Attend:	Attend:		Attend:	Attend:
Read:	Read:		Read:	Read:
Watch:	Watch:		Watch:	Watch:
Discuss:	Discuss:		Discuss:	Discuss:
Turn in:	Turn in:		Turn in:	Turn in:

Source: Adapted from Fisher, D., Frey, N., & Hattie, J. (2020). *The distance learning playbook, grades K–12: Teaching for engagement and impact in any setting.* Corwin.

For now, let's focus on the learning intentions and success criteria. In simultaneous learning, learners are more than likely working toward the same learning intentions and success criteria. Therefore, we must ensure that we communicate these learning intentions and success criteria so that regardless of the context, learners are aware of the what, why, and how of learning.

The key point here, one that we have observed to be quite powerful in ensuring clarity in simultaneous learning, is that we have to blend together tools from instructional technology with different ways of communicating clarity. There are many ways that we can communicate the *what*, *why*, and *how* of learning to our students (see Almarode et al., 2021). For example, if learners are engaged in asynchronous learning, simply posting the learning intention and success criteria will not be enough for communicating clarity around complex concepts, skills, and understandings. Likewise, learners who are face-to-face today and at a distance tomorrow may need additional support and scaffolding beyond what was provided in the classroom. Too narrow a focus on learning intentions and success criteria will lead to a decline in rigorous and engaging learning experiences in simultaneous learning. This does not have to be the case. Simultaneous learning does not mean we avoid collective learning, concept attainment, guided-inquiry, project-based learning, and problem-solving teaching. Let's look at other ways of developing and communicating clarity that support simultaneous learning.

> **SIMPLY POSTING THE LEARNING INTENTION AND SUCCESS CRITERIA WILL NOT BE ENOUGH FOR COMMUNICATING CLARITY AROUND COMPLEX CONCEPTS, SKILLS, AND UNDERSTANDINGS.**

➡ *I can statements:* This approach is the most popular but may not always be the most effective means of implementation. *I can* statements are explicit and direct statements about what, why, and how for simultaneous learners.

➡ *We can statements:* These explicit and direct statements take a collaborative view on learning. Rather than what individual learners must do, this form of clarity highlights the value of collective learning and what learners and teachers are expected to do together. This can include Google Docs, Jamboard, or breakout rooms.

➡ *Checklists:* While not a recipe or collection of agenda items, checklists provide the essential components of the learning intention. In some cases, checklists are presented in the form of questions that encourage self-reflection, self-monitoring, and self-evaluation during simultaneous learning.

➡ *Holistic/analytic rubrics:* Rubrics provide learners with the expectations for process, task, or product along with descriptions of the level of quality for each expectation.

➡ *Single-point rubrics:* Rather than different levels of quality, a single-point rubric provides the expectations for mastery in a process, task, or product. In other words, only a single level of quality for each expectation.

➡ *Teacher modeling:* Helping learners understand expectations for learning can come from us modeling the content, practices, and dispositions. This modeling would allow learners to see the learning in action. Learners would use the model to guide their own work toward the learning intention.

> ➜ *Exemplars*: We can provide worked examples and/or exemplars of processes or finished tasks or products. Worked examples would provide a comparison for learners to use in their own work, while exemplars would possess all of the expectations for success and truly be a model for their learning path.
>
> ➜ *Student created*: The final way to implement clarity is by co-constructing those expectations with learners. The process of co-constructing is a collaborative effort between teachers and students as they set the criteria for success before engaging in the work.

When we blend these different approaches for communicating clarity with the instructional technology tools available to us in today's world, we can differentiate the communicating of clarity based on the context. Figure 1.6, on the next page, provides specific examples of ways to crosswalk between the planning templates for simultaneous learning and the implementation of that clarity.

One important observation about the approaches for synchronous and asynchronous learning is that the artifacts generated for these two groups can and will likely be helpful to face-to-face learners when they have questions, and we are not immediately available. For example, if a face-to-face learner in Ms. Marquez's classroom begins working on a free-response item during an asynchronous practice assessment, this learner can return to the recording of the worked examples and review the Google Doc containing the success criteria for such a response. Remember, simultaneous learning does not mean double the workload. Instead, we are bringing together what works best in each context and leveraging to move learning forward.

WITHOUT CLARITY IN LEARNING, WE ARE MORE LIKELY TO HAVE FRAGMENTED LESSONS AND BUSY WORK.

Clarity ensures that the focus is on the learning within any context by providing scaffolding and support as learners transition from face-to-face to distance learning. But again, student clarity comes from teacher clarity at the onset of developing and communicating learning expectations. Clarity sets the stage for engagement, synchronous and asynchronous task design, ensuring the right level of challenge, and monitoring student learning. If we are to effectively engage our learners in core ideas, support their development of specific skills, and facilitate their understanding of complex concepts, we have to be intentional, deliberate, and purposeful in how we develop and communicate learning expectations. Without clarity in learning, we are more likely to have fragmented lessons and busy work where learners simply log on, complete some (perhaps random) task, and log off. Without clarity from both the students and teachers, all other decisions in simultaneous learning rely on hope and luck, neither of which are evidence-based tasks or strategies, and ensure that this particular learning context is both stressful and impossible. Clarity about learning really narrows our teaching and learning focus so that we engage in rigorous learning that makes efficient use of the available tools and is effective in moving learning forward.

Now, let's take a closer look at asynchronous and synchronous learning before bringing them back together and focusing on the designing and implementation of simultaneous learning.

1.6 EXAMPLES OF DIFFERENT APPROACHES TO COMMUNICATING CLARITY IN SIMULTANEOUS LEARNING

	I Can/We Can Statement	Checklist	Analytic or Holistic Rubric	Single-Point Rubric	Teacher Modeling	Worked Examples	Co-Construction
Face-to-Face Learning	Introduce at the beginning of the mathematics lesson and respond to student questions. Put visual examples beside each statement to support language development.	Provide a hard copy of the essential elements of their still-life drawings for learners to glue into their sketchbooks. Each student has a supply box that is for their use.	Provide a rubric through a hyperlink in the narrative writing assignment description using Google Docs.	Provide a laminated single-point rubric to learners for use during their math talk.	Model or demonstrate the process for balancing chemical equations at the beginning of the block, and co-construct an anchor chart of the criteria for success.	Using cooperative learning, have learners compare and contrast different student responses to free-response items on the world history assessment; develop a group list of success criteria.	Lead a whole-group discussion based on an exemplary CAD drawing. Using Google Docs, develop a class set of success criteria.
Synchronous Learning	Provide a digital version of the I can/We can statements for learners to have on their screen.	Use a digital interactive notebook and provide this checklist as a hyperlink and/or digital download.	This can be the same as the face-to-face group.	Provide a digital copy of the single-point rubric along with a short video clip modeling how to use the single-point rubric.	Share your screen and animate the process in your slide deck; pause at multiple locations for synchronous learners to "raise their hand" to ask and answer questions.	Use the document camera to share your screen. Develop a reflective question template in Google Docs that learners must complete with a face-to-face learning partner.	Use the interactive whiteboard feature in your online platform; have all learners log into Zoom so that Zoomies and Roomies can see and interact with each other.
Asynchronous Learning	Provide a chart on the online platform that aligns the learning intention, success criteria, and tasks.	Create a narrated slide deck using Loom that breaks down the checklist for learners; hyperlink the checklist in the slide deck. Link this to your online platform.	While this can be the same as the face-to-face group, have face-to-face peers use Flipgrid to explain different elements of the rubric to their peers. We simply monitor their clips as they prepare them and suggest edits and revisions.	Same as synchronous learning. Simply provide a link to the video clip on the online platform.	Use PlayPosit to build an interactive video that pauses and asks the asynchronous learners questions about your modeling; link to the video clip on the online platform.	Simply record what you did for your synchronous learners. Make this available on your online learning platform.	Record this session and share with a link on your online learning platform; as an additional task, ask asynchronous learners to make additions, edits, or suggestions to the list provided through Google Docs.

2 ASYNCHRONOUS LEARNING

In this section:

Recall from our previous discussion of terminology that asynchronous learning can occur in any geographic location. Teachers provide a learning progression and the necessary resources for students to engage in the learning at their own pace and time. While there are time limits and due dates on this progression (i.e., one week to complete the tasks or "by the end of the day"), students are responsible for accessing the information on a digital learning platform as well as managing their own time and pace within the time limits and before the due dates. When engaged in asynchronous learning, Ms. Lewanowicz's and Ms. Marquez's learners are neither Roomies nor Zoomies. They are engaged in an essential part of simultaneous learning that lays the foundation for synchronous and face-to-face learning.

With the many variants of schooling that have emerged in 2020, perhaps no aspect of instruction has shifted as much as asynchronous learning. In the past, it was relegated to two forms: independent practice in the classroom and homework. For many of us, our in-class practice work was often cognitively less demanding so that we could turn attention elsewhere in the classroom (e.g., work one-on-one with students, address other needs with learners). What seemed to be most valued was that a task could soak up a student's attention without requiring much of the teacher's time.

MANY STUDENTS DESCRIBE THEIR HOMEWORK AS BEING 'BUSYWORK' WITH LITTLE UNDERSTANDING OF THE PURPOSE. THAT'S ON US.

This approach to out-of-class work came with unintended side effects. Our out-of-class work (homework) can become too cognitively demanding. A MetLife (2008) survey of teachers found that 26 percent of secondary teachers confessed that they often or very often assigned homework when they ran out of time for class. Obviously, this approach is not a sound pedagogy when our learners are asked to practice something they have not been taught. Alternatively, many students describe their homework as being "busywork" with little understanding of the purpose. That's on us. In other words, there is a gap in clarity about the learning. In simultaneous learning, we must make sure we communicate the value and importance of asynchronous learning if we are to successfully design and implement rigorous and engaging experiences that move learning forward for both Roomies and Zoomies. This demands that we move away from the limited view of asynchronous learning as an opportunity to independently practice and toward asynchronous learning as a prime opportunity to preview and review.

This belief by students that asynchronous learning is of little value to them works against our efforts to move to split day, A–B, and full week simultaneous learning schedules. Given the reduced live instructional minutes available for synchronous learning, flipping the classroom is a reasonable choice. The flipped classroom is a hybrid design that foregrounds initial content learning in advance of synchronous or face-to-face instruction. The asynchronous portion of a flipped classroom is usually comprised of direct instruction, short lectures, or demonstrations that introduce students to a new skill or concept. This inverted model of instruction places a premium on student collaboration and teacher facilitation of learning that follows in the synchronous or face-to-face context. However, students who don't engage in the asynchronous prework are disadvantaged when it is time to apply knowledge in a synchronous context. Rather than focusing on differentiated teacher supports during application, instructional time must be used instead to get students caught up on what they missed.

The schooling experiences of the last year hold the potential to change some of that resistance to preview and review. Students' digital competencies have grown and so have teachers' ability to create asynchronous learning experiences in more creative and effective ways. Teachers have used asynchronous learning days to remind students to practice mindfulness and other social-emotional learning tenets. Students can also use asynchronous learning time to work through a Webquest, follow the art teacher's video to create their own artistic work, or even learn an 8-count of dance steps. But to do so requires that students know why asynchronous learning is crucial for them and an essential part of the learning experience or task.

THE VALUE OF PREVIEW AND REVIEW IN LEARNING

Modeling (preview) is the demonstration of a concept or skill through direct instruction; practice (review) is the application of what has been initially learned. Learners need a clear and coherent model of the concept and skill to begin to develop an understanding of how that particular concept or skill is defined. Returning to our discussion about clarity for learning, two dimensions of clarity have to do with the quality of explanations and examples. However, we have long understood that learning does not occur through exposure alone. Simply letting information wash over a student does not ensure that they will encode, store, and then be able to retrieve that information later on. Both Roomies and Zoomies need opportunities to apply the knowledge they are acquiring and consolidating so that what they learn is durable, flexible, and usable beyond a single learning experience or task. Some situations that ask learners to apply their learning promote initial short-term learning, such as repeating information, responding to questions in the moment, and writing notes. Other situations that ask learners to apply their learning are more sophisticated and include consolidation of concepts and skills through compositions and projects. Asynchronous learning has the potential to do both. To capitalize on this potential, we must view asynchronous learning experiences and tasks as opportunities to preview and review. Let's look at **preview techniques** as initial instruction and **review techniques** for application.

If practice (review) is one bookend on the asynchronous bookshelf, then modeling (preview) is the other. Practice is made more productive when students have a clear idea of what success looks and sounds like. The direct instruction and demonstrations you provide form a visual and aural model for the student to emulate. Having said that, keep in mind that opportunities to practice are layered into preview as well as review learning.

> BOTH ROOMIES AND ZOOMIES NEED OPPORTUNITIES TO APPLY THE KNOWLEDGE THEY ARE ACQUIRING AND CONSOLIDATING.

PREVIEW: BUILDING KNOWLEDGE

The advent of virtual instruction has opened up new possibilities for teachers like Ms. Lewanowicz, Ms. Marquez, and the teachers in Sanchez ISD. In full-time distance learning, many teachers began to record short videos of themselves. They posted these videos on their learning management systems and soon learned that their value extended

SET UP A "PLAYLIST" OF VIDEOS WE HAVE RECORDED AND ORGANIZE THEM INTO CATEGORIES SO THAT STUDENTS CAN REFER BACK TO THEM.

beyond initial instruction. Students accessed these demonstration videos when they needed them and did not have to rely on recall alone to remember the details. Families reported that these videos served as guidance for them when assisting their child, which in these situations was a Zoomie. As children return to classrooms for partial days, don't abandon this approach. This approach is very important in scaffolding the learning of our Roomies as well. We can set up a "playlist" of videos we have recorded and organize them into categories so that students can refer back to them when they need additional explanations or examples related to a particular learning experience or task. Keep in mind that a naming convention for the videos is important so that learners in either context can go directly to the specific clip. Simply supplying the date of the recording is not helpful. For example, instead of "Monday_subtraction examples," maybe "two-digit by two-digit regrouping." Or, we might set up a playlist called Writing Processes and include video demonstrations labeled Drafting, Revising, and so on. Look at the usage reports, too, to find out which students are referring back to the videos as it can give you further information about who you may need to check in with to see if they are experiencing difficulty in a particular content area, skill, or understanding.

DEMONSTRATING THINKING

Teacher modeling. Teacher modeling is one approach to use for asynchronous demonstration lessons. Thinking is invisible, but when a teacher models decision-making about abstract processes, students are better able to understand how conditional knowledge is utilized. Consider any of the tutorials you've tuned into in order to learn how to prepare dumplings, perfect your dance moves, or use a new educational technology tool. The best ones don't just show you how to do something; they explain their thinking at each stage of the process. When developing videos, we can use a think-along technique (a running commentary on your thinking) as part of our modeling. Through our work with schools, we found that first-person *I* statements work better than second-person *You* statements, as the former invites students in, while the latter is directive and distancing to both Roomies and Zoomies. This spoken language mirrors one's own internal dialogue. These *I* statements can feel awkward at first, but they contribute to a think-along's effectiveness by triggering empathetic listening on the part of the student. Our human nature is to respond emotionally to such statements. Consider the difference between these two approaches:

➡ *First-person statement*: "Hmm . . . I'm seeing a word I don't really understand. I'm going to reread the sentence to see if I can make sense of it."

➡ *Second-person statement*: "When you run into a word you don't know, reread the sentence."

The first example gives students insight into the use of a reading comprehension strategy. The second, while good advice, uncouples the strategy from the decision to use it. Novice learners do not just need to know what the strategy is—they need to know when to apply it in their own learning. We use the following guidelines (Fisher, Frey, & Lapp, 2009) to plan and record robust think-alongs about a passage of text, a skill, or a process.

➡ Name the strategy, skill, or task.

➡ State the purpose of the strategy, skill, or task.

➡ Explain when the strategy or skill is used.

➡ Use analogies to link prior knowledge to new learning.

➡ Demonstrate how the skill, strategy, or task is completed.

➡ Alert learners to errors to avoid.

➡ Assess the use of the skill.

Direct instruction. Another technique for asynchronous demonstration lessons is direct instruction. With an effect size of 0.59 (www.visiblelearningmetax.com), direct instruction offers a pedagogical pathway that provides our learners with the modeling, scaffolding, and practice they require when learning new skills and concepts. Rosenshine (2008) noted that the structure of a direct instruction lesson should follow a pattern that we have adapted for asynchronous learning:

➡ Begin the lesson with a short review of previous learning. Going from the known to the new is powerful.

➡ Begin a lesson with a short statement of goals.

➡ Present new material in small steps, providing practice for students after each step. This can be accomplished by using pauses for students to reply. For instance, saying "Repeat after me" encourages students to engage.

➡ Give clear and detailed instructions and explanations.

The second part of direct instruction can be implemented when our students are in synchronous learning (Zoomies) or face-to-face learning (Roomies). We must ensure that we communicate that we will continue with this learning when they are logged in to the online platform or back in the classroom:

➡ Continue the lesson by providing a high level of **active and deliberate practice** for all students.

➡ Ask a large number of questions, check for student understanding, and obtain responses from all students to make their thinking visible.

➡ Guide students during initial practice, removing scaffolds that are in place as they develop in their proficiency.

Once students have gained an initial understanding and have acquired the necessary skills to successfully engage in independent practice, we can provide additional opportunities for this practice through asynchronously learning (i.e., the review dimension of asynchronous learning).

NOVICE LEARNERS DO NOT JUST NEED TO KNOW WHAT THE STRATEGY IS—THEY NEED TO KNOW WHEN TO APPLY IT.

INTERACTIVE VIDEOS IN ASYNCHRONOUS LEARNING

Videos have long been used in educational settings to build knowledge around various topics and skills. However, a significant barrier to learning through video is the passive nature of video viewing. For Ms. Lewanowicz, her use of video to provide background knowledge of Ancient Greece, Rome, and Egypt must move beyond simply sitting and watching an extended clip. While the content of the video may be of value and tightly aligned with the specific standard, there is usually little application required by the learner. They simply sit and watch. Interactive videos make it possible to interleave rehearsal and retrieval of information during the video. Regular rehearsal and retrieval are crucial for learning new information, and repeated use consolidates learning and improves retention of that information (Roediger & Karpicke, 2006). Retrieval requires learners to actively recall information and not just passively let it settle there after the initial learning. The more times learners engage in retrieval practice in any context, the more likely the information becomes permanent.

RETRIEVAL REQUIRES LEARNERS TO ACTIVELY RECALL INFORMATION AND NOT JUST PASSIVELY LET IT SETTLE THERE.

So, what are interactive videos? Interactive videos are interspersed with questions that pause the video until the student responds to the questions. The effect size for interactive videos is 0.54 (www.visiblelearningmetax.com)—the potential for this asynchronous tool to accelerate learning makes interactive video worth the effort. Most programs, such as PlayPosit, EdPuzzle, and Nearpod, allow us to either create our own recording or use a second-party video that aligns with our learning intentions and success criteria. A feature of many interactive video programs is that they can be linked so that incorrect answers take the student to the section of the video when the concept was discussed or even to another source for additional background knowledge. When Ms. Marquez uses interactive video in her U.S. government class, her students' responses are logged into a database so that she can review both her learners' responses and the number of attempts for each student per question. This is valuable information for designing and implementing the next learning experiences or tasks in synchronous learning (i.e., distance or face-to-face). We will talk more about this in the next chapter. For now, consider these tips for making the most of your interactive videos:

- Limit the overall length of the video to about six minutes (less for younger students).
- Set the purpose of the video using a statement of the learning intention and success criteria. Teachers in Sanchez ISD provide the learning intentions and success criteria at the opening of the video and then review them at the conclusion of the video.
- Remind students of materials they may need, including items for taking notes.
- Build in three to five questions to pace the video lesson. These questions should align with the learning intentions and success criteria.
- Use both multiple-choice and open-response questions.

➡️ Make sure that you are asking questions that are consistent with the depth of knowledge (DOK) required to understand the content. Ask questions that cause them to think critically and reflect. Again, these should align to the type of thinking and reflection in the learning intentions and success criteria. If Ms. Marquez wants her learners to explain the balance of powers, an open-response question that requires an explanation is best.

➡️ Ramp up their ability to monitor their own learning by inviting them to answer the questions as an initial assessment. At the end of the video, they can compare their initial responses and post a reflection on their learning.

The assessment data that interactive videos yield is a valuable tool for gauging the progress of students in asynchronous learning. Use the data to identify areas in which some or all students are confused. Consider allowing students to repeat the videos multiple times to "beat their score." This encourages practice and allows you to determine where the errors were on the first view versus subsequent views.

REVIEW: APPLYING KNOWLEDGE

Ms. Lewanowicz, Ms. Marquez, and the teachers in Sanchez ISD now turn to the application of the content, skills, and understandings acquired during the preview phase of asynchronous learning and the synchronous and face-to-face learning experience or task. The application of knowledge comprises the other half of asynchronous learning. Students need to practice what they are expected to learn, retrieve, and transfer. But this practice is not just any practice. Let's start by making an important point: practice that is deliberate is not mindless repetition. Deliberate practice, a concept introduced by Ericsson and colleagues (1993), is intentional and requires feedback. The intentionality of this practice is directed to where the learner needs additional practice. However, without a mental model of what success looks like, the effects of practice are greatly diminished. After all, most of us can testify to failed practice of a musical instrument or sports drills that did not yield much improvement. Time devoted to practice alone is not the secret sauce. When goals, feedback, and a model are in place for our learners' deliberate practice can have an accelerating influence on learning. Goals for our learners include improvement on the number of correct answers on a low-stakes assessment, increased reading fluency rate, or accurate completion of a timed assignment, just to name a few examples. With an effect size of 0.79 (www.visiblelearningmetax .com), it is worth incorporating into the instructional flow.

> PRACTICE THAT IS
> DELIBERATE IS NOT
> MINDLESS REPETITION.

In addition, the effects of deliberate practice are enhanced when practice opportunities or sessions are spaced into shorter intervals rather than amassed in one long session, often described as cramming. Many of us learned the travails of trying to cram for a

test the night before it was administered rather than distributing study time across the week. These two principles, related to deliberate practice, should guide our design and implementation of asynchronous learning:

 Pace the timing of deliberate and asynchronous practice sessions so that they are shorter in duration but more deliberate. There are many asynchronous learning tools that allow us flexibility in what tasks are assigned to our learners (e.g., IXL, Reflex, Achieve3000). This feature helps us make practice more deliberate for our learners.

Set improvement goals with students and provide feedback on their efforts. Small group learning and scaffolding, two topics we will unpack in the next chapter, allow us to set these goals and provide the feedback needed for effective asynchronous learning. This is a key connection between what happens with our Roomies, Zoomies, and then during asynchronous learning.

Goal setting is crucial for motivation and as an assessment tool. Encourage students to set goals for deliberate practice and track their "personal best" records. For instance, students can set their personal best goals to accurately identify sight words, the number of books and articles read, or the number of words written during timed writing assignments. When giving students formative feedback, discuss the students' "personal best" attainments and review their growth trajectory on quizzes and tests.

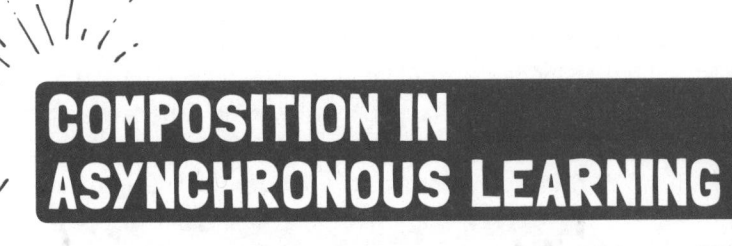

COMPOSITION IN ASYNCHRONOUS LEARNING

Composition through extended writing often occurs asynchronously. With the already limited amount of synchronous and face-to-face instructional time, it may not be a wise use of instructional minutes during simultaneous teaching. However, as a means for assessing student understanding, it is invaluable. Composition requires marshaling lots of skills, especially for planning, monitoring, and purpose. Composition can include short constructed responses or longer essays. In each case, we must make sure we are teaching the expectations of the writing. In addition, we must also closely examine our own construction of the prompt we have furnished, as a poorly constructed prompt can lead students away from what we really want from the writing task.

MAKE SURE WE ARE TEACHING THE EXPECTATIONS OF THE WRITING.

A suitably designed writing prompt should guide students in developing their essays. As such, the basic components of a writing assignment or prompt are as follows:

1. The topic
2. The audience
3. The rhetorical structure or genre to be produced

Therefore, our asynchronous writing tasks should ensure that our students are able to parse a writing assignment such that they can answer the following questions:

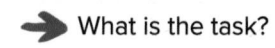 What is my purpose for writing this piece?

Who is my audience?

What is the task?

A good writing assignment or prompt should lend itself to this type of student analysis.

To guide our use of composition tasks in asynchronous learning, there are resources that support our formulation of a prompt that incorporates the three previous questions. The Literacy Design Collaborative (www.LDC.org) proposes that good writing prompts can be formulated using prefabricated task templates that allow the teacher to customize them for learners. For example, the following **argumentation task template** invites students to compare two conditions:

[Insert question] After reading _____ (literature or informational texts), write a/an _____ (essay or substitute) that compares _____ (content) and argues _____ (content). Be sure to support your position with evidence from the texts.

This template can be used as a springboard for writing in any number of subject areas. In each case, the writing task specifies the purpose and task in detail. Ms. Lewanowicz and Ms. Marquez often use video clips to walk learners through the writing prompt, in addition to providing written instructions on their learning management system (e.g., Canvas). We have augmented these prompts with explicitly stated information about audiences in order to further support students as they craft their pieces:

➡ Third Grade: <u>Do you think words can set you free?</u> Read <u>Pat Mora's poem, "Words Like Confetti."</u> Use evidence from the text and your own personal experiences to write an opinion <u>for or against the power of words for your classmates. Do they really have the ability to do everything Mora says?</u> Be sure to use evidence to support your opinion.

➡ Middle School ELA: <u>How can decisions affect a life?</u> After reading the chapter <u>"The Last Shot"</u> in Kwame Alexander's *The Crossover*, <u>write a defense for the boys of Josh's decision to play in the championship game and JB's decision to go to the hospital to see his father.</u> Be sure to support your <u>defenses</u> with evidence from the text.

➡ ELA: <u>What is courage in a time of war?</u> After reading <u>Stephen Crane's</u> *Red Badge of Courage*, write an <u>essay for peers</u> that compares <u>Henry Fleming's inner conflict as he wrestles with moral and ethical issues of war</u> and <u>argues for a definition of true courage.</u> Be sure to support your position with evidence from the text.

➡ U.S. History: <u>What is the cost of freedom?</u> After reading *Korematsu v. United States*, <u>323 U.S. 214 (1944), the Supreme Court decision upholding the internment of Japanese and Japanese Americans during World War II</u>, write an <u>essay for fellow high school history students</u> that compares <u>the cases brought by the plaintiff and defendant</u> and argues <u>whether the court ruled rightly or wrongly on its constitutionality</u>. Be sure to support your position with evidence from the text.

➡ Science: <u>Is the expense of interplanetary exploration worth the cost?</u> After reading the article, <u>"Mars Rover Curiosity's Siblings: A Short History of Landings on Alien Planets" by Clay Dillow</u>, write a <u>fact guide for potential voters</u> that compares <u>the knowledge gained with the cost in doing so</u> and argues <u>its worth to humankind</u>. Be sure to support your position with evidence from the text.

INTERACTIVE DIGITAL NOTEBOOKS IN ASYNCHRONOUS LEARNING

If there is one thing we will never stop using across any school setting, it is the interactive digital notebook. These are not the physical spiralbound notebooks we used to have students carry, but rather digital slides that visually resemble journals. What both digital and spiralbound notebooks have in common is that they provide a way for learners to organize and record their learning in an asynchronous environment.

IF THERE IS ONE THING WE WILL NEVER STOP USING ACROSS ANY SCHOOL SETTING, IT IS THE INTERACTIVE DIGITAL NOTEBOOK.

For the interactive digital notebook, the teacher designs a template for the student notebook, including a table of contents, learning intentions and success criteria for the unit, and materials needed for assignments. Kasey Woollard, a high school biology teacher from Sanchez ISD, organized hers to include multiple units of instruction (see Figure 2.1).

Each student has their own digital interactive notebook and can access it through their own devices, as well as keep the notebook stored on their own learning management site. Learners can keep all their writing assignments in one location. This is advantageous for the teacher and the student. The materials do not get lost or left behind at home or school (a significant problem for simultaneous learners), and the teacher can easily review and comment on their work in a digital space. A digital notebook also allows for teachers and students to record audio as another form of demonstrating understanding. For example, Ms. Woollard added to her students' digital interactive notebooks a task for answering questions as they watched an interactive video on adaptations for the gecko's feet (see Figure 2.2). A resource for templates that you can use is slidesgo.com/school.

2.1 DIGITAL INTERACTIVE NOTEBOOK

Name: YOUR NAME HERE

Class: Biology: Semester 1

Unit 1: Introduction to Biology

Unit 2: Cellular Processes

Unit 3: DNA and Genetics

Image source: yaophotograph/iStock.com

2.2 DIGITAL PAGE FOR COMPOSITION IN SCIENCE

| 1. 2 Gecko Feet | 🔖 to divider |

Instructions: Watch the Gecko Feet video and answer the questions below.

Video Questions	My Response
1. How do geckos' feet stick and unstick so quickly?	*Geckos' feet stick and unstick so quickly because _____.*
2. What did Tanya, a student in Robert Full's lab, need to figure out before she could answer her question?	*Tanya needed to figure out _____.*
3. What did Anne, one of Robert Full's graduate students, discover about spiders?	*Anne discovered that spiders _____.*
4. What is the name of the gecko-inspired robot built by the Stanford group?	*The gecko-inspired robot is called _____.*
5. Do you think animal research is important? Explain.	*I do/do not think animal research is important because _____.*

Image source: piola666/iStock.com

Keep these things in mind as you design an interactive digital notebook for your class:

➡ *Start small if this is your first time.* Design one for a single unit of instruction so you can gain some experience in finding out what works best for your students.

➡ *Organization is key.* Develop a table of contents and provide links to assignments and materials. This makes finding assignments and materials much easier for learners.

➡ *Get feedback from your students* about how they are experiencing success and where they are having difficulty. Make sure you are teaching how to navigate your digital notebook. You might consider making a playlist of short videos that students and families can refer to.

A two-column *t*-chart can be used to provide students an opportunity to describe what they know and how they can show what they know. The know/show chart should be based on the success criteria and invite students to reflect on what they have learned and how they can demonstrate their learning. Analyzing the "know" column allows you to identify which ideas stuck with your students. The "show" column provides students with opportunities to propose alternative assessment methods. The artwork below is a sample from an elementary school student.

ASYNCHRONOUS ORAL RETELLINGS

When students retell a book, article, video, or passage, they provide us with evidence of their use of academic language as well as their comprehension. An oral retelling is an original account of the text or experience. If the oral retelling is drawn from a narrative text, we are listening for their use of story grammars, including plot sequencing, character development, and themes. If it is an informational text, then a quality retelling should include a logical and accurate representation of the information. An oral retelling is not a blow-by-blow description of everything that happened (listen to a young child telling you everything about a movie, punctuated with "and then . . . and then . . ."). Rather, retelling should be concise, accurate, and include learners' own insights and conclusions about the text.

AN ORAL RETELLING IS NOT A BLOW-BY-BLOW DESCRIPTION OF EVERYTHING THAT HAPPENED.

Oral retellings have long been recognized as a means for supporting the understanding of the reader, as it is common for students to gain new insight during the act of retelling. However, the limitations of listening to a child retell a story in a busy face-to-face classroom has meant that teachers don't collect as many as they would otherwise like.

Asynchronous oral retellings have created a space for teachers to assess progress more frequently while at the same time students are consolidating their understanding about what they have written. Students record their retelling on a time-limited video platform such as Flipgrid and submit it to the teacher. Younger students can also use SeeSaw. These recorded retellings are invaluable as an assessment, to be sure. They can also be shared in parent–teacher conferences to show families past and current performance.

As with other asynchronous learning tasks, we must set aside time to teach students about retelling before assigning them to independently engage in this task. A rubric is a great tool to use to support initial teaching. As one example, there is an informational retelling rubric in Figure 2.3.

2.3 INFORMATIONAL TEXT RETELLING RUBRIC

	Proficient—3	Adequate—2	Needs Attention—1
Main ideas	Main ideas are identified. Examples are given to illustrate these ideas.	Most main ideas identified. Examples are less descriptive.	Overlooked main ideas essential to the text. Few or no examples or descriptions of main ideas offered.
Supporting details	Supporting details are clearly connected to the main ideas.	Supporting details are identified but are not told in association with main ideas.	Few or no supporting details offered.
Sequence	Sequence of retelling is accurate and reflects the order used by the author.	Sequence is similar to order in book, with some instances of "doubling back" during retelling.	Sequence is difficult to discern.
Accuracy	Facts are relayed accurately.	Retelling is mostly accurate, with few errors.	Retelling is inaccurate.
Inferences	Student makes connections within text (e.g., meaning of title; usefulness of information).	Student makes few associations between pieces of information in text.	Student makes no associations within text.

Source: Fisher, D., Frey, N., & Hattie, J. (2017). *Teaching literacy in the Visible Learning classroom, grades K–5*. Corwin.

Once we have set aside time to initially teach this skill, using the above rubric to support this learning, we can then transition to a single-point rubric that learners can use to guide their retelling when they are engaged in the task asynchronously.

Ms. Lewanowicz links the rubric to her learners' retelling task so that they can self-reflect, self-monitor, and self-evaluate their own work (see Figure 2.4).

2.4 SINGLE-POINT RUBRIC FOR INFORMATIONAL TEXT RETELLING

Shines	Success Criteria	Refines
	I identify the main idea and give examples to support my thinking.	
	I use supporting details that are clearly connected to the main idea.	
	My retelling is accurate and reflects the order used by the author.	
	My facts are accurate.	
	I make connections within the text (e.g., meaning of title; usefulness of information) during my retelling.	

In this specific example, the *shines* column represents those aspects of the retelling that meet or exceed the success criteria. The *refines* column represents those areas that need more deliberate practice or additional instruction.

Single-point rubrics foster the self-assessment habits of students. When they understand the success criteria, they can monitor their progress and make adjustments in learning. This also changes your role from the decider of students' learning to one that is a validator or challenger as you discuss evidence that students use to determine their progress. These tools also give you a more robust means of assessing student progress and providing feedback. View single-point rubrics as a dialogue between you and the student to ask further questions and confirm or revise the student's perceptions of self as a learner.

ASYNCHRONOUS PRACTICE TESTS

Formative practice testing, in which students take short quizzes to understand their command of the subject or topic, is an effective way to check for understanding while also prompting deliberative practice in an asynchronous environment. Formative practice tests are not part of the student's grade, as the emphasis here is on practice to

gain self-knowledge of learning gaps where additional learning or practice is needed. A meta-analysis of the effectiveness of formative practice testing on advancing student learning reported these findings (Adesope, Trevisan, & Sundararajan, 2017):

→ Lots of practice tests didn't increase student learning. One is often enough.

→ Feedback paired with the practice test enhances learning.

→ The usefulness of practice tests was strong at both the elementary and secondary levels.

→ The value of formative practice tests is in students reflecting on their results.

THE GOAL IS FOR STUDENTS TO MONITOR THEIR LEARNING AND MAKE PLANS FOR ATTAINMENT.

We have all taken practice tests. Perhaps it was to prepare for your driver's license exam or for a college entrance test. We can make them a part of our asynchronous learning by providing a short representative practice assessment a week before the end-of-unit exam. These can be a combination of multiple-choice and short constructed answers but should align with key concepts that will be assessed at the end of the unit. However, the most significant and important component of practice testing is that our learners interpret the results. In an asynchronous learning environment, we can provide a process and structure that allows our students to indicate which answers are correct and incorrect, challenge them to sort out their responses to identify what they have mastered, what they need to practice, and where they need additional instruction. The goal is for students to monitor their learning and make plans for attainment. An example of a practice test analysis template is in Figure 2.5.

2.5 PRACTICE TEST ANALYSIS

Complex Items I Got Wrong		Complex Items I Got Right	
Foundational Items I Got Wrong		Foundational Items I Got Right	
What did I do well?	What do I need to practice?	What do I still need someone to teach me?	What can I teach others?

Source: Adapted from Fisher, D., Frey, N., Bustamante, V., & Hattie, J. (2020). *The assessment playbook for distance and blended learning: Measuring student learning in any setting.* Corwin.

Practice tests are another tool for assessing student progress toward success criteria. The results of practice tests provide you with information about skills and concepts that may need to be revisited in advance of an end-of-unit evaluation. Practice test results also highlight the needs of individual students who may continue to hold misconceptions or partial understandings that are interfering with their mastery of the topic.

ASYNCHRONOUS PROJECT-BASED LEARNING

Project-based learning (PBL) describes an extended inquiry process and is an umbrella term used to describe a multitude of instructional models, including design-based learning and Genius Hour. Each of these approaches has specific processes that are utilized, but all are done in a spirit of inquiry and draw on more than one discipline. PBL builds expertise precisely because it requires students to use knowledge in unique ways. These projects and problems can be addressed in a multitude of ways, such that no two projects or solutions are identical. In fact, the appeal of inquiry-based approaches is that the investigation is just as important as the outcomes or deliverables. These projects offer further opportunities for students to set goals, monitor their progress, reflect on their learning, and apply strategic thinking to arrive at solutions. Some PBL projects are driven by a broad essential question that doesn't seek a solution but rather is meant to open the door for investigation.

Projects traverse the boundaries of synchronous and asynchronous learning. Some elements of a project, including teaching about content, as well as research and investigation processes, are going to occur in a live environment. But other elements, including conducting the investigation and writing about it, can be accomplished asynchronously. That said, students should have prior experience in doing so with you as a guide before doing so independently. The Buck Institute for Education (Buck Institute, 2021) offers these considerations for conducting PBL in virtual learning:

PBL BUILDS EXPERTISE PRECISELY BECAUSE IT REQUIRES STUDENTS TO USE KNOWLEDGE IN UNIQUE WAYS.

- ➡ Provide students with datasets and readings that students can use for their project.

- ➡ Curate websites for students to find reliable and accurate information, rather than turning them loose on the internet.

- ➡ When possible, design projects that allow them to draw on the knowledge of family members, such as interviewing them about an event in history or exploring their family's experiences.

- ➡ Create daily and weekly schedules and timelines to help students stay on track and foster self-management skills.

- ➡ Provide ample time during simultaneous instruction for students to provide each other feedback and to revise under your guidance.

ASYNCHRONOUS TEACH-BACK

A valuable and motivating asynchronous learning experience is teach-back. We first began exploring this in distance learning as a different way of gauging student understanding. In teach-back, a student is assigned a skill or concept the class has been learning. Their challenge is to record themselves teaching it to others in one to two minutes. Young children, as an example, might teach a sibling about a math skill they are learning. Older students might summarize important points to keep in mind to avoid plagiarism, calculate the area of a triangle, or assemble a dissection kit. An immediate outcome is that it promotes knowledge retention through verbalization.

Defining the audience is key. Make sure your students know that they are not addressing you but rather their classmates. Teach students about peer response, and have students view teach-back videos of your classmates. These should always be vetted by you first, as you don't want to perpetuate inaccurate examples. These become yet another valuable assessment tool for you, as you can monitor progress and identify when reeteaching needs to occur. Like all assessment information, these serve as feedback to you about the impact of your instruction.

IT'S BEEN A HIDDEN GIFT THAT WE ARE THINKING WITH MUCH MORE INTENTION ABOUT THE ROLE OF ASYNCHRONOUS LEARNING FOR THE PURPOSES OF PREVIEWING AND REVIEWING CONTENT.

> Teach-back is used widely in the health-care field with patients. Near the end of a visit, the patient is asked by the health-care provider to "teach back" the information shared. ("Just to make sure I'm clear, can you show me how you will use the inhaler?"). The purpose of teach-back is two-fold: to reinforce complex information for the patient and to assess the patient's understanding. This check for understanding is feedback to the health-care provider about the clarity of their instructions.

Asynchronous learning can be more than mindless repetitions and homework. In fact, it has become a crucial dimension of learning in split day, A–B, and full week schedules. It's been a hidden gift that we are thinking with much more intention about the role of asynchronous learning for the purposes of previewing and reviewing content. In fact, because we must call out specific times in schedules when it occurs, we are thinking more closely about what we want our students to accomplish during that time. By virtue of doing so, we can be clear about how we can best utilize the precious synchronous learning time we have in simultaneous learning. And that is the subject of the next chapter.

3 SYNCHRONOUS LEARNING

In this section:

- ☐ CREATING OPPORTUNITIES FOR DIALOGUE AND ACADEMIC DISCOURSE
- ☐ SET THE STAGE FOR LEARNING
- ☐ SYNCHRONOUS COLLABORATION WITH PEERS
- ☐ COLLABORATIVE LEARNING
- ☐ COACHING AND FACILITATING IN SYNCHRONOUS LEARNING
- ☐ DIFFERENTIATING LEARNING EXPERIENCES BASED ON LOCATION

Recall that synchronous learning involves instruction and interaction live, in real time. Some learners are at home, at the local Boys and Girls Club, or any other location, but still participating in live instruction. At the same time, other students are in the physical classroom with their teacher. For Ms. Lewanowicz, her students log on for morning meetings starting at 8:30 a.m. and then have several synchronous sessions throughout the day. In the split day model, Ms. Marquez has all of her students engaged in synchronous learning every morning. If asynchronous learning is about preview and review, synchronous learning is about engaging and connecting, not just attending. For us to capitalize on synchronous learning, we must

1. Create opportunities for dialogue and academic discourse around concepts, ideas, and essential understandings

2. Encourage collaboration, cooperation, and interaction among all learners, especially between Roomies and Zoomies

3. Provide scaffolded learning experiences and tasks that build learners' capacity for successful asynchronous learning

CREATING OPPORTUNITIES FOR DIALOGUE AND ACADEMIC DISCOURSE

Dialogue and academic discourse are essential in developing understanding of concepts and ideas. For learners to successfully engage in this dialogue and discourse, they must have multiple opportunities to see this type of academic talk modeled for them and then be able to practice identifying and using academic language across multiple contexts. Synchronous learning provides both us and our learners a platform to build academic language, model and facilitate dialogue and discourse, and create opportunities for learners to engage in this dialogue and discourse among themselves.

If the outcome is to promote dialogue and academic discourse, that must be modeled for Roomies and Zoomies. Over time, students assume more responsibility for their own dialogue and discourse, moving from being participants in a modeled lesson to apprentices in shared instruction, to collaborators with their peers in breakout rooms, and then to independent performers during their asynchronous learning experiences.

SET THE STAGE FOR LEARNING

As we discussed in Chapter 1 on clarity, communicating the learning intentions and success criteria are crucial for launching the lesson. These may be posted on your learning management system, and you may have also recorded them for asynchronous lessons. Having said that, we suggest doing the following:

➡ Revisit these so that students have clear direction about where the lesson is headed.

➡ Take the time to parse both and pose open-ended questions to students to warm up their use of academic language.

➡ Remember that providing learning intentions doesn't simply mean rattling off the goal. For example, you might say something like this: "I want to make sure I'm being clear, so can someone explain in their own words where we're headed today?" Then listen to determine whether further clarification is needed.

Another decision point for you to make is whether you will be including demonstration in your synchronous lesson. These demonstrations, which can include direct instruction, teacher modeling, or lecture, are sometimes done asynchronously. Examples of these are in the previous chapter on asynchronous learning. However, in other cases, you may choose to provide a demonstration lesson synchronously because you specifically want to promote discourse and dialogue. For instance, a more complex topic may require incremental steps, frequent checks for understanding, and the potential for slowing down or speeding up instruction. In those cases, it makes sense to shift a demonstration to the synchronous learning environment. Many video conferencing software used for synchronous learning has a built-in reaction button to inform the teacher when a student needs the lesson pace to slow down.

Modeling should be based on the learning intentions and success criteria, as well as provide students a mental example they can call upon when they are asked to complete tasks in another phase of instruction. Questioning can be a feature, but its point is primarily to activate students' background knowledge. For example, Ms. Marquez might ask students to talk about the role of citizens in a representative democracy compared to a pure democracy. In synchronous learning, she would provide a list of terms or key ideas that would be used to talk about civic engagement and democracies. Ms. Lewanowicz would model the use of academic language by engaging in think-alouds, shared readings, read-alouds, lectures, and other whole-class events with her third graders. After modeling, students can reflect on what they learned both through writing independently and talking with a partner. These partners could both be Zoomies assigned to a specific breakout room or a Roomie, logged into Zoom while sitting in the classroom, partnered with a Zoomie.

Synchronous learning experiences offer time for students to participate as partners and enable them to internalize the interactive format as well as the information that is being learned. Over time, students will develop the ability to perform these tasks independently; these early-phase exchanges provide them with time to practice in supportive situations that encourage them to use academic language to own and share their thoughts and developing understanding.

SYNCHRONOUS LEARNING EXPERIENCES OFFER TIME FOR STUDENTS TO PARTICIPATE AS PARTNERS.

Assessment begins at the start of a synchronous lesson. After introducing the learning intentions and success criteria, pause to give students an opportunity to self-assess. Use the poll function to invite students to rate their relative level of confidence or their background knowledge about the topic. This gives you valuable information at the onset about how to proceed.

SYNCHRONOUS COLLABORATION WITH PEERS

In this phase of synchronous learning, students have opportunities to work together while the teacher monitors their progress and provides support when needed. Dialogue and academic discourse take center stage as students work together in classroom structures such as a jigsaw task. They talk about tasks and ideas, and they question one another. They negotiate meaning, clarify their own understanding, and strive to make their ideas comprehensible to their peers.

Peer discussion can happen in the main room of a synchronous session, with Roomies and Zoomies equally contributing. However, there can be a reluctance to participate as students worry about inserting themselves into a conversation and interrupting someone else. This leads to lots of silences where no one wants to talk. In simultaneous learning, this can be even more awkward, as the Zoomies are at a disadvantage in gaining the floor. Teach your Roomies and Zoomies some basics about how to do so. You've probably noticed that radio reporters manage not to interrupt one another despite the fact that they can't draw on any visual cues from the other speaker, such as facial expressions and hand signals. Instead, they use a technique we've come to call "radio talk." They use each other's names to signal when they are entering and ending their comments. You can teach your students to state your name and then their own: "Mr. Fisher, Arif." That allows you to facilitate the discussion and serve as a buffer to make it easier for students to engage in authentic discussion.

Teach your students about wait time, too, so that they are aware of your rhythms in facilitating whole and small group discussions. Wait times need to be longer during synchronous learning due to audio delays. This is especially important when simultaneous teaching is happening, as Zoomies can be further disadvantaged when the Roomies hear the question first. When you ask a question, remind them to pause before responding to give the Zoomies a chance to catch up. When engaged in simultaneous discussions, mark certain questions specifically for a group ("Here's an idea I've been wondering about, and I'd like to hear from students online first.").

WAIT TIMES NEED TO BE LONGER DURING SYNCHRONOUS LEARNING DUE TO AUDIO DELAYS.

It's also useful to have some spotlight practices to shape discussions. Spotlight practices are discussion protocols that you return to time and again because of their versatility. Students don't need to be continually challenged to learn new discussion protocols, as their focus becomes enacting the process rather than on the content they are supposed to be learning. Identify three to five evergreen discussion protocols that are enduring and flexible and teach them. In short order, you'll simply have to remind students of the protocol they are using. It results in less time spent giving instructions and more time on instruction.

See It/Say It. The use of imagery can be a powerful way to spark an authentic discussion. Jessie Engstrand teaches world history and uses a strategy she borrowed

from her primary-grade colleagues: See It/Say It. The teacher projects an image for the students to see. The Zoomies have it in their chat via file transfer, and the Roomies have it on the second screen. There are, of course, other ways to provide students access to images. In this case, the image was of World War I soldiers in a trench, some of them wearing gas masks. Ms. Engstrand invites students to verbalize what they see. She provides them with several possible sentence frames that they can use:

➡ I see a _____ and it makes me think/remember _____.

➡ I wonder if _____.

➡ In this image, there is _____.

Ms. Engstrand alternates between Roomies and Zoomies, with each knowing that they will have a chance to share. As more students share, the focus becomes on details, and students naturally make connections with the texts they have been reading. The point of these tasks is to build oral language skills, background knowledge, and vocabulary while providing students visual information rather than only auditory input.

Arif says, "I wonder why they don't have any trench art. We read about that, so I thought that there would be some."

Izzy adds, "In this image, there are some people who have on masks. I wonder why they are not all wearing masks. It reminds me of the times today. Not everyone wears their mask."

The conversation continues, and students are asked to focus on the emotions that they see in the image. Ms. Engstrand asks them to name the emotions that they see in the faces of the people in the image, as well as the emotions they experience as they look at it. Later, she asked them to think about what might have happened before this picture was taken and offers additional sentence frames.

THIS APPROACH WORKS WELL FOR FULLY SYNCHRONOUS LEARNING (I.E., ALL ZOOMIES) AND IN SIMULTANEOUS LEARNING (I.E., ROOMIES AND ZOOMIES).

Close the assessment loop on See It/Say It by having students compose a short, constructed response about the image they have discussed. Ask them to use evidence from the visual to support their assertions. They should include key vocabulary that was used during the discussion.

Discussion roundtable. Another strategy for supporting dialogue and academic discourse in peer collaboration is the use of a discussion roundtable. This approach works well for fully synchronous learning (i.e., all Zoomies) and in simultaneous learning (i.e., Roomies and Zoomies). As we mentioned earlier, if we have both Roomies and Zoomies, we can have our Roomies log on to the distance learning platform and use earbuds when interacting with Zoomies. This allows us to put all of our learners into breakout rooms and, at the same time, promote interaction between both groups. A discussion roundtable uses a Frayer model to encourage learners to seek and summarize the ideas of their peers (see Figure 3.1).

 FRAYER MODEL FOR FOCUSED INSTRUCTION DISCOURSE AND DIALOGUE

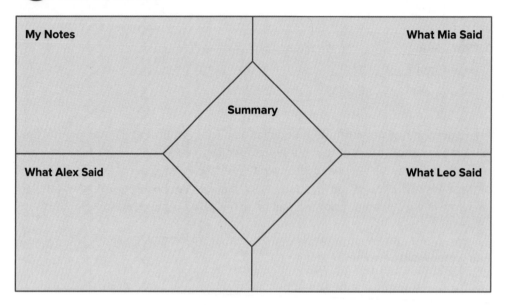

➡ During breakout rooms, learners share their thoughts about specific concepts and ideas (e.g., civic engagement and democracy in Ms. Marquez's class).

➡ Peers then summarize what each individual shared in the breakout room.

➡ To close the discussion roundtable, each learner pulls together everyone's responses and creates their own individual summary.

TO GENERATE EVIDENCE OF LEARNING, THE DEPARTMENT AGREED TO REQUIRE STUDENTS TO VIDEO RECORD THEIR CONVERSATIONS AND SUBMIT THEM.

Learners can take a picture of their discussion roundtable and submit the image through the learning management system. Another option is to complete this task using Google slides or another comparable collaborative platform. In this situation, Ms. Marquez can monitor the notes created by each group and join the breakout rooms when feedback is needed.

Completed discussion roundtable documents are a valuable assessment tool. There is accountability to the group in terms of documenting their collaboration. More importantly, these graphic organizers provide you with evidence about their academic understanding and growth over the course of the interaction. Focus your assessment eye on quadrant 1 ("My Notes"). This gives you initial assessment information about the student's early understanding of the reading before they began their peer discussion. Compare that to their summary at the end of the interaction. Are you seeing a qualitatively improved understanding? Are there misconceptions still being held? The initial and postassessment information it yields assists you in gauging their progress.

Virtual reciprocal teaching. Reciprocal teaching is a Roomies and Zoomies task that promotes dialogue and academic discourse among peers (Palincsar & Brown, 1984). During this particular task, synchronous learners are assigned a comprehension strategy: predicting, summarizing, clarifying, or questioning. Each group stops at predetermined times to share their thinking using the strategy that they have been assigned. Again, this can be implemented with both Roomies and Zoomies, ensuring that both groups have the opportunity to interact with each other.

The high school teachers from Sanchez ISD make use of reciprocal teaching to shape their dialogue and academic discourse in ninth-grade English classes as they read *Lord of the Flies*. The English teachers developed and shared documents with their students that include stopping points for their discussions. To generate evidence of learning, the department agreed to require students to video record their conversations and submit them through the learning management system adopted by the district. The department adopted a rubric produced by the Teaching New Literacies group to provide students feedback about their discussion (see Figure 3.2).

Importantly, using reciprocal teaching allows for the English Department in Sanchez ISD to scaffold their students' learning. Through the submitted videos and the rubrics, teachers are able to provide a range of scaffolds and move their students' learning forward.

> USING RECIPROCAL TEACHING ALLOWS FOR THE ENGLISH DEPARTMENT IN SANCHEZ ISD TO SCAFFOLD THEIR STUDENTS' LEARNING.

3.2 **INTERNET RECIPROCAL TEACHING DIALOGUE RUBRIC**

RT Strategy	Beginning—1	Developing—2	Accomplished—3	Exemplary—4	Score
Questioning	Generates simple recall questions that can be answered directly from factors or information found within the website's home page.	Generates main idea questions that can be answered based on information gathered by accessing one or more links to the website's content.	Generates questions requiring inference. Facts and information must be synthesized from one or more links to the website's content and combined with prior knowledge.	Generates questions flexibly that vary in type, based on the content read and the direction of the dialogue.	
Clarifying	Identifies clarification as a tool to enhance understanding and initiates clarification dialogue when appropriate.	Identifies appropriate words for clarification with the dialogue's context.	Assists group in clarifying identified words based on context clues.	Uses strategies for word clarification that can be applied generally across reading contexts.	

(Continued)

(Continued)

RT Strategy	Beginning—1	Developing—2	Accomplished—3	Exemplary—4	Score
Summarizing	Summary consists of loosely related titles.	Summary consists of several main ideas but also many details.	Summary synthesizes main ideas, is complete, accurate, and concise.	Summary is accurate, complete, and concise, incorporating content vocabulary contained in the text.	
Predicting	Demonstrates knowledge of predictions as an active reading strategy.	Directs group predictions to set a clear purpose for reading.	Articulates predications that build logically from context.	Provides justification for prediction and initiates confirmation or redirection based on information located in text.	

Source: Teach New Literacies, https://teachnewliteracies.wordpress.com/internet-reciprocal-teaching/

You don't have to analyze students' virtual reciprocal teaching recordings for the entire school year. Once they have had foundational experiences using your feedback to their groups, transform the expectations so that they are assessing themselves. Turn this rubric into a single-point rubric. Isolate the column that signifies proficiency (Accomplished) and place it in the center. Add a blank column to the left (Shines) and another to the right (Refines) so that students can self-assess.

COLLABORATIVE LEARNING

In essence, jigsaw is an approach in which synchronous learners are members of two different groups: a home group and an expert group. Each time they meet with a group, there are different purposes and tasks. Over the course of the jigsaw, students deepen their understanding of the content-area text and have opportunities to develop and practice their communication and social skills. The effect size of jigsaw is 1.20 (www .visiblelearningmetax.com)—super powerful when done well. There are many ways to implement the jigsaw, but it's key that students talk with others during the process. Indeed, it was not created for online learning (it was invented in the arts) but works very well in synchronous learning environments, especially in engaging and supporting dialogue and discourse between Roomies Bend Zoomies. To be clear, a jigsaw is not just divide-and-conquer reading in which the text is divided up and students tell each other what they read. For example, consider the following implementation of a jigsaw by Sanchez ISD teacher, Mathew Snyder.

The students in Mr. Snyder's algebra 2 class were asked to read from their digital mathematics textbook. This particular chapter focused on the different ways to solve systems of equations (e.g., elimination, substitution, graphing, and with technology). Let's look at the steps he took to engage both his Roomies and his Zoomies:

Step 1: All learners, even those in face-to-face learning, logged in to Zoom. Mr. Snyder created named breakout rooms that served as expert groups (e.g., elimination, substitution, graphing, and with technology). In their **expert groups**, each student had been assigned the same section of the chapter—a particular way to solve systems of equations. They read this section, prepared to teach this particular approach, and were asked to consider several questions:

➡ What do you not understand or are confused about?

➡ What makes sense to you?

➡ What do you want to know more about?

They shared their responses to these topics with other members of their expert groups in a breakout room. They collaborated to ensure that each member of the group had a working knowledge of the section of the text they had been assigned.

Step 2: Each member of the group had been assigned a letter, and when the timer was up, Mr. Snyder regrouped students so that all of the *G*s were together, all of the *J*s were together, all of the *K*s were together, and all of the *L*s were together (he selects random letters so that students don't think that they are in the *A* group). The students were each asked to join their unique chat room and share with the others in their new (**home**) group their thinking about their assigned section. They had to model and teach how to solve systems of equations using elimination, substitution, graphing, and technology. Their peers, who had not read that section, took notes, highlighted, completed practice problems, and added digital comments to that section. They specifically talked about what made sense and what did not. The purpose was to summarize the big ideas. If a teacher wanted to kick up the use of digital resources for this lesson, they could also use some virtual math manipulatives such as DeltaMath, Desmos, or CanFigureIT.

Step 3: Students returned to their original **expert groups** or chat rooms and reported back what they learned in step 2. They talked about how their approach fits with the big idea of solving systems of equations. They looked for similarities and differences and other relationships between the approaches.

Step 4: In this case, Mr. Snyder added another step and invited each group to report what they learned to the whole class. Mr. Snyder also could have then asked them to do a task that used the knowledge and understanding they had derived from this first round—as at a minimum, all students had been exposed to the main ideas, engaged and heard content, knew subject matter vocabulary, and had been introduced to the four approaches to solving a system of equations. A visual representation of Jigsaw appears in Figure 3.3.

JIGSAW IS NOT JUST DIVIDE-AND-CONQUER READING.

3.3 USING A JIGSAW ARRANGEMENT

Phase One: Expert groups

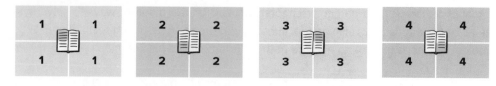

Phase Two: Home groups

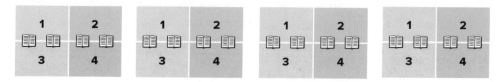

Phase Three: Return to expert groups

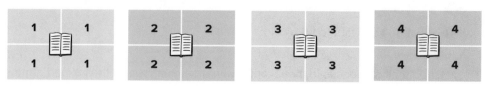

Source: Fisher, D., Frey, F., Lapp, D., & Johnson, K. (2020). *On-your-feet guide: Jigsaw, grades 4–12.* Corwin.

Discussion circles. Collaborative learning discussions incorporate academic language as a necessary means of focusing on and delving deeper into content. This is particularly important for English learners, as it provides an opportunity to practice and learn academic language (Frey, Fisher, & Nelson, 2013). As we like to say, "You don't get good at something you don't do." If English learners are not using language, they're probably not learning language.

> IF ENGLISH LEARNERS ARE NOT USING LANGUAGE, THEY'RE PROBABLY NOT LEARNING LANGUAGE.

Another approach that supports learners in engaging in dialogue and academic discourse is the use of specific roles in collaborative learning tasks. We can implement discussion circles during synchronous learning using breakout rooms. A discussion circle is a strategy that assigns specific roles and tasks related to a specific chunk of content (Wilfong, 2009). Although the size of each discussion circle varies and ultimately is up to the teacher, we have found that breakout rooms of up to five students are most effective. Figure 3.4 provides examples of discussion circle roles and tasks and includes discussion directors, summarizers, word wizard, mapmaker, and highlighter (Wilfong, 2012). The roles used in a specific discussion circle depend on the nature of the content and the objectives for that particular lesson. Keep in mind that a student can also have more than one role.

3.4 DISCUSSION CIRCLE ROLES AND TASKS

Discussion Circle Role	Task
Discussion director or leader	Direct, lead, or guide the activities in the discussion circle breakout room. Decide the presentation order for each group member and their task. Develop a set of critical thinking questions (not yes, no, or one-word response questions) that encourage group members to make connections between the content, current events, other class topics, and/or group members' lives.
Big idea builder or summarizer	Develop a list of the big ideas or the "must-knows" for the content using Google Docs or some other interactive software. Create a visual or written summary of the content (for example, you can use a Popplet to capture, organize, and help visualize ideas). Prepare a response to the question "Why is this material important?"
Word wizard	Identify key vocabulary, terms, or concepts. Prepare a description of each vocabulary term or concept (you can use vocabulary.com to assist with definitions and pronunciations). Create a visual for each item (you can use Wakelet, Pear Deck, or another tool). Identify a specific example of each item. The word wizard provides locations or further information about each vocabulary, term, or concept.
Map maker	Create a concept map of the material (you can use Canva, for example). Explain why certain concepts are connected together on the concept map. This should be uploaded to the learning management system so that each group member can access the document later.
Highlighter	Identify important readings, sections, or passages. Mark these passages with an electronic sticky note or tab (you can use OneNote to clip information into your notebook so you can annotate). Justify why particular readings, sections, or passages were selected.

Source: Adapted from Wilfong, L. G. (2009). Textmasters: Bringing literature circles to textbook reading across the curriculum. *Journal of Adolescent & Adult Literacy, 53*(2), 164–171, and Wilfong, L. G. (2012). The science text for all. Using textmasters to help all students access written science content. *Science Scope, 35*(5), 56–63.

Once students are assigned to groups and their individual roles are determined, the teacher should provide ample time for the completion of individual tasks. How students are grouped is ultimately up to us. However, research suggests that students should be grouped using a variety of criteria (e.g., interests and strengths) and have the opportunity to work in different groups throughout the school year.

Take a reading assignment in any class (e.g., a chapter on classification in biology, a section on periodic trends in chemistry, a section on matrix operations in algebra, or the section on the geometric representation of polar coordinates). Once students have an explicit purpose for reading, they are more likely to engage in the reading task. Then do the following:

1. Preassign groups of up to five students. Create these breakout rooms prior to the synchronous learning experience.

2. Within each group, assign students their individual roles or empower students to select a role. More experienced students can decide on roles themselves.

3. Identify the content that is the focus of the discussion circle (e.g., reading selection, concept, topic, idea, or problem set). Ensure these resources are available on the learning management system.

4. Provide time for students to individually complete the task associated with their role. This can also be done asynchronously or before learners are assigned to breakout rooms.

5. After a period of time, students take turns presenting their tasks to their peers in the breakout room.

Just as the English Department from Sanchez ISD decided to gather video evidence of their learners' reciprocal teaching, discussion circles can be recorded, and artifacts collected to provide insight into student learning. Once they have become more experienced with discussion circles, shift the focus to self-assessment.

> COACHING AND FACILITATING FOCUSES ON GUIDING STUDENTS' THINKING WHILE AVOIDING THE TEMPTATION TO TELL THEM WHAT TO THINK. THIS REQUIRES THAT TEACHERS ASK THE RIGHT QUESTION TO GET THE STUDENT TO DO THE WORK.

COACHING AND FACILITATING IN SYNCHRONOUS LEARNING

Synchronous learning time includes small group specialized instruction. These teacher-led dialogic events are intended to stretch learning using more complex instruction. A hallmark is the use of scaffolds that deepen the cognition and metacognition of the students. During these events, teachers elicit student talk as a way to figure out what students know and what they still need to know. This is an opportunity for teachers to use questions, prompts, and cues to help students complete tasks. The name of this instruction move is important: The teacher's role is to coach and facilitate learning, not engage in extensive direct instruction (which occurs during demonstrations).

The particulars of scaffolding, coaching, and facilitating should be informed by the assessment information teachers glean from these interactions: What do students understand, not understand, or partially understand? Although this type of instruction is teacher led, it does not mean that students are not talking to each other in the main room or in breakout rooms. They use talk to ask questions—of the teacher, of peers, and of themselves. They use language to clarify understanding, provide feedback to a partner, and reflect on their learning. Essentially, this aspect of the learning focuses on guiding students' thinking while avoiding the temptation to tell them what to think. This requires that teachers ask the right question to get the student to do the work and teach the students how to ask powerful questions. Questioning has an effect size of 0.48, and scaffolding has an effect size of 0.58 (www.visiblelearningmetax.com).

We are impressed with Marty Nystrand and colleagues' (1998) notion of the "uptake" question where teachers (or students) validate particular student ideas by incorporating their responses into subsequent questions; and by "authentic" questions whereby questions are asked to obtain valued information, not simply to see what students know and don't know. These authentic questions are questions without "prespecified" answers, and like uptake questions, they also aim to contribute to coherence.

When questions fail to ensure success, teachers can rely on prompts and cues. In general, prompts are statements made by the teacher to focus students on the cognitive and metacognitive processes needed to complete a learning task. Metacognitive strategies have an effect size of 0.55 (www.visiblelearningmetax.com). When teachers provide prompts, the students apprentice into cognitive and metacognitive thinking.

For example, sixth-grade teacher Yusuf Dhagah said to a group of students during their synchronous session, "I'm thinking of the video we watched that showed what life was like when the pyramids were being built." In this case, he provided a background knowledge prompt. Later, he said, "I'm thinking about what we don't yet fully understand and what we can do to figure things out," which is a reflective prompt focused on metacognition.

Cues, on the other hand, are designed to shift a student's attention. Sometimes, students need this level of support to work through something that is confusing. For example, Missy Stein was working with a group of students, and they seemed to miss the exponent in the problem. She used the highlight function on the virtual whiteboard to shift her students' attention to that part of the problem, and it worked. As one student said, "OMG, I totally missed that. I thought it was a mixed fraction and it's an exponent." Again, the teacher does not simply tell the student what to think but rather shifts the learner's attention to something that is likely to help.

In addition to lessons that rely on questions, prompts, and cues to address errors and misconceptions, there are times in which teachers meet with groups of students for coaching, based on their identified learning needs, and provide instruction. For example, a group of students in Maria Sandoval's English class did not provide evidence in their writing. She met with them during one of their remote learning days to provide coaching about this necessary part of the task while the Roomies worked on revising their papers.

In other cases, these sessions are less focused on the specific academic content that students need to learn and are more focused on social skills, communication skills,

> THERE ARE TIMES IN WHICH TEACHERS MEET WITH GROUPS OF STUDENTS FOR COACHING, BASED ON THEIR IDENTIFIED LEARNING NEEDS.

or interpersonal skills. For example, Angela Jung noticed that some of her students were not reaching a consensus about the ideas in the text they were reading. She took notes while watching their video and scheduled a time to meet with them. As part of the coaching session, she provided the students with a recorded example from another group (with their permission) and asked what they noticed from observing these other students.

"They listen better than we do," Adam said.

Toby added, "Yeah, and they talk one at a time. Also, they were able to get the work done pretty fast. We take forever, and it's not always really good when we're done."

"I like how they compromised," Sarah said. "They got to a good place, and they could all support it."

"What do you think you could try so that your group meetings are more productive?" Ms. Jung asked.

The students shared ideas and Ms. Jung made a list. After several minutes, she shared her screen, adding, "I think that this summarizes your ideas. Can you take a minute and review my notes so we can revise or add to them?"

The students did, and their conversation continued. Over time, they reached agreement and committed to trying out their new plans. They each took a picture of the screen and promised to have that open the next time they met. At the end of their meeting, Ms. Jung said, "I hope you are proud of yourselves, and I look forward to your future conversations. These are really good skills to build; they're important in a lot of contexts."

Later, reflecting on the experience, Ms. Jung said, "The interesting thing about distance learning is time. Some groups need a lot more time and others need less time. In my physical classroom, everyone has to stop at the same time so that we can go on with the lesson. In distance learning, if a group takes two hours to reach a consensus and develop their product, it's totally fine. The point is that they're learning."

ONE BENEFIT OF SEE IT/SAY IT IS THAT IT STRENGTHENS VOCABULARY.

Earlier in this chapter, we described a process called See It/Say It. This same process can be used for English learners as well as young learners. One benefit of See It/Say It is that it strengthens vocabulary. When learners have a concept, providing them a label (word) is easier. For example, first-grade teacher Amelia Torres showed a group of her Roomies a drawing of a person giving a speech to a large group. As they discussed the image, they got to learn the terms *podium, audience, backstage*, and *cast*. In addition, they built background knowledge as students talked about what it might feel like to be on the stage (fear, excitement, nervousness) and what happened before the image was created, from something as simple as climbing stairs to get on the stage to getting ready to speak to the audience.

Essentially, teachers can meet with small groups to provide additional learning, using scaffolding, coaching, and facilitating, based on their needs. Given the physical constraints of the classroom and the distancing that is required, teachers often assign a task for Roomies and then log in to provide this type of lesson for the Zoomies. These lessons tend to be short and focused on specific skills or concepts that students still need to learn. For example, Javier Espinoza met with two of his third-grade students who were experiencing difficulty decoding words. He used virtual letter tiles (www.real lygreatreading.com/lettertiles) to engage his students in decoding words. He reminded students of the short vowel sounds and then created a consonant–vowel–consonant pattern. At one point, he had the letters *d* and *g* with a yellow tile in the middle. He asked students to read the words as he moved each vowel into the place of the yellow tile. As he did, he prompted and cued them. Later in the lesson, he had the letters *m* and *p* with a yellow tile between them and asked students to write each word on their board in either the "real word" column or the "not a word" column. When they showed him their work, he was able to scaffold for students when they used the incorrect sounds.

DIFFERENTIATING LEARNING EXPERIENCES BASED ON LOCATION

Much of this chapter has been about creating cohesive learning experiences for Roomies and Zoomies. But there may be times when you want to differentiate learning experiences based on students' location. For instance, you might need some time for some small group instruction through coaching and facilitating, and all of the students you need to see are in the physical classroom. Or perhaps you are spending time administering diagnostic assessments and plan to accomplish this on a rotating basis as students attend the physical classroom. The online students can still interact with one another in meaningful ways.

THERE MAY BE TIMES WHEN YOU WANT TO DIFFERENTIATE LEARNING EXPERIENCES BASED ON STUDENTS' LOCATION.

Sara O'Conner's third graders are learning about animals and biomes. The Zoomies have time each day for a week to learn about a selected animal and prepare to teach the whole class. One group has selected blue whales. At designated times each day, they are learning from home; the Zoomies are in their breakout groups while the Roomies are working with their teacher in the physical classroom. The students also have time during their asynchronous learning to engage in research and develop their slides. They use their breakout room time to plan the lesson and to make sure that they do not repeat information. Ms. O'Conner has provided students with a checklist that they can use to design their lessons, and they know that they will be teaching from home to the whole class (see Figure 3.5).

On teaching day, the whale group is ready. Andrew starts by reminding his peers that they need to have something to write with. He says, "You need your paper and pencil or your laptop with the notes open so that you can write down important ideas." Brianna shares next, saying, "Our learning intention today is 'We are learning about blue whales and their biome.' We have two success criteria. One, I can tell another person about the life of blue whales, what they eat, and where they live. Two, I can compare blue whales and their life to another animal that another group teaches you about."

From there, each student discusses information about blue whales while Cassidy advances the slides. The students have a number of pictures that they share while they discuss their important ideas and details. They also show video clips of whales breeching and talk about the various body parts and how those parts are useful in survival. Throughout their presentation, the students invite their peers to respond in the chat, use emojis, and raise their hands to ask clarifying questions. After six minutes, Jacob announces a thirty-second stretch break, which he leads. When they return, Angel takes over and shares information about the potential extinction of blue whales, mainly due to vessel strikes and entanglements in fishing gear. Angel asks his teacher to send everyone to breakout rooms for three minutes so that they can talk about the best thing that they learned. Roomies put on their headphones and are paired with a Zoomie to have these partner conversations. When the class returns, Andrew asks the students to create a Know/Show chart to document their learning. The entire lesson is fifteen minutes long.

3.5 CHECKLIST FOR CLASS LESSON

☐ **Learning intention**

☐ **Success criteria**

☐ **Main idea from each student**

☐ **Supporting details from each student**

☐ **Checks for understanding after each presenter**

☐ **Knowledge check at the end**

Know/Show charts, discussed in the previous chapter, provide valuable feedback to you about what students know and are able to do. They also allow students choice in assessments. Choose one item on their Know/Show chart for further use as an individual assessment.

TOO OFTEN, STUDENTS HAVE NOT HAD THE COLLABORATION AND SCAFFOLDING NECESSARY TO BE SUCCESSFUL OUTSIDE OF SYNCHRONOUS OR FACE-TO-FACE LEARNING.

Learners who successfully engage in academic talk build self-esteem through competence in dialogue and academic discourse—talking about their learning. Self-efficacious learners drive their own motivation to engage in asynchronous learning. Confident learners are more likely to complete independent and asynchronous tasks because they know they can complete them successfully. Too often, students have not had the collaboration and scaffolding necessary to be successful outside of synchronous or face-to-face learning. But those who have completed this instructional cycle learn from experience that independent learning is fully in their power.

Now, let's put asynchronous and synchronous learning together with face-to-face learning by setting up an environment conducive to simultaneous learning.

4 ROUTINES AND PROCEDURES THAT INTEGRATE SYNCHRONOUS AND ASYNCHRONOUS LEARNING

In this section:

- ☐ GETTING TO KNOW SIMULTANEOUS LEARNERS
- ☐ ESTABLISHING NORMS, PROCEDURES, AND PROCESSES
- ☐ NORMS FOR INTERACTING IN SIMULTANEOUS LEARNING
- ☐ LINK NORMS TO CLASS AGREEMENTS
- ☐ DEVELOP AND TEACH ORGANIZATIONAL PROCEDURAL ROUTINES

Let's bring this all together—the combination of teaching some learners at a distance and others face-to-face learning in the same learning experience found at the intersection of asynchronous learning, synchronous learning, and face-to-face learning. Learners will walk or log into our classrooms having previewed or reviewed content, skills, and understandings during asynchronous learning. What happens next requires that we are clear about norms, procedures, and processes for the successful interaction between us, our synchronous learners, and our face-to-face learners. Some of these norms, procedures, and processes are things we took for granted in the past: starting times, gathering and readying materials, asking questions, working with peers, etc. To be honest, we have to revisit our "first day of school" checklist when initiating simultaneous learning.

GETTING TO KNOW SIMULTANEOUS LEARNERS

IN SIMULTANEOUS LEARNING, WE HAVE TO GET TO KNOW OUR STUDENTS IN A DIFFERENT WAY.

First and foremost, we must strive to foster, nurture, and sustain a positive student–teacher relationship with each of our learners. When we first transitioned to a distance learning model, those learners started the year or semester in our classrooms. We had the opportunity to get to know them. Since then, we have started a new school year with students we did not have the chance to get to know in a face-to-face learning environment. This makes simultaneous learning different. We have to get to know our students in a different way. While this is a key component of any classroom, the fact that some of our learners will be at a distance, maybe for the entire quarter, semester, or year, necessitates that we are sure to "get to know" them just as well. Students' interests are a key lever for building relevancy into learning, as students with a higher degree of interest in a topic are more likely to perform at higher levels (Palmer et al., 2016). Having said that, "interest" isn't likely to manifest itself as a purely academic pursuit. We can't imagine a student breathlessly saying, "I can't wait to learn about trigonometric identities." But a student might have the dream of one day becoming a marine biologist, an air traffic controller, a paramedic, or a contractor. These interests likely compel the learner to read and talk about those careers. Thus, an entry point into trigonometry might be connecting these concepts, skills, and understandings to the use of radar in directing airplanes or the planning and building of a house.

Developing an interest survey that learners complete in either asynchronous or synchronous learning can provide valuable information in ensuring we can reach and teach our Zoomies. Successful interest surveys and interviews use language that is developmentally appropriate. For younger students, this may include graphics that allow for ease of response. Older students can complete open-response questions that give them the opportunity to answer in their own words. Many teachers construct their own surveys to tailor them to the specific content area and topic.

Before administering the survey, discuss the purpose with your students. As we discussed in Chapter 1, clarity applies here as well. Simultaneous learners must know the purpose of the survey and clearly understand that it is not a test. Ms. Lewanowicz and Ms. Marquez take the survey first. If you decide to do so, tell them about your responses after they have completed their own interest surveys so that you don't influence their answers. After administering the surveys, construct a chart to note the results. Look for items students have in common with one another. These insights can serve as a means to foster positive peer relationships when using collaborative or small group learning during synchronous learning. Use the results to recommend readings, assign preview and review tasks, and make connections to course content during asynchronous learning. There is a tremendous opportunity to forge a positive teacher–student relationship by telling a student, "I read this and I thought of you." You can capitalize on student interests by drawing them into topics being taught. For instance, a student who is interested in theater or the performing arts might be interested in how Shakespearean drama was performed during a particular historical time period. Don't limit connections to academic content. Ask a student who is interested in karate about their next belt test or what coda they are working on. In high school chemistry, we can connect the concept of viscosity to why we must change the oil in our cars.

When our learners are here (in the classroom) and there (on the screen), we have to approach our fostering, nurturing, and sustaining of relationships a bit differently. Making an authentic and genuine effort to get to know them should be one of our first tasks in simultaneous learning.

ESTABLISHING NORMS, PROCEDURES, AND PROCESSES

Simultaneous learning requires us to consider the typical rituals in our classroom. Do you greet students at the door? Have you prepared your classroom so that it has been customized for them? Do they see their names on their desks? Do you have a birthday wall? Are there organizational systems in the room so that students know where to find materials, submit work, and get help? Simultaneous learning needs the same structures, but in two different locations: at a distance and face-to-face.

A simultaneous classroom plan is a teacher-created document that captures the norms, agreements, procedures, and schedules that will be used by Roomies and Zoomies. Experienced teachers may long ago have internalized their classroom management plan, but simultaneous learning requires some rethinking about what works well for you and your students. Committing a thoughtful and well-constructed plan to paper is a first step in a proactive approach to simultaneous learning and can prevent problems from emerging as learners transition between asynchronous, synchronous, and face-to-face learning. For example, which group of students starts first, the Roomies or Zoomies? Trying to launch class with both groups at the same moment is stressful and sometimes counterproductive. Giving yourself a few minutes to settle one group and then welcome the other seems to be more effective. Being proactive, not reactive, is key to creating an environment that is conducive to learning. Learning environments without a holistic approach to the learning environment have more instances of negative student–teacher interactions and less time spent on academic instruction (Conroy et al., 2008).

Start with our vision of what an ideal learning environment would look like in simultaneous learning. What are your views and beliefs about how teaching and learning should occur for Roomies and Zoomies? What are your beliefs concerning community and diversity? Keep your audiences in mind—if you are teaching very young children, offer an appropriate version for your students. In addition, families who speak a language other than English appreciate your effort to communicate in the home language. If you are not fluent in the home language, seek assistance from your school's parent resource coordinator, parent center, or district language office for translation. This is an investment that is well worth the time.

The norms, agreements, procedures, and schedules for simultaneous learning should strive to create a learning environment that best matches our views on teaching and learning—do not let simultaneous learning dictate who we are as a teacher. Instead, take what worked well for us in a face-to-face learning environment and leverage available tools to create that type of environment in simultaneous learning.

Once the classroom management plan has been constructed, you can produce a child-friendly version for students and families. Post this on your learning management system (LMS) and share it digitally with families. This is recommended for two reasons: It serves as an initial means for communicating with students and families, and it can become a tool for discussion when a difficulty does arise with a specific student or students.

NORMS GOVERN HOW ROOMIES AND ZOOMIES INTERACT WITH ONE ANOTHER.

NORMS FOR INTERACTING IN SIMULTANEOUS LEARNING

Our Roomies and Zoomies will interact with us and each other according to the norms that have been agreed upon. The interesting thing is that groups will adopt their own norms whether they are formally named or not. We have all witnessed this phenomenon countless times when you have met an established group for the first time. Furthermore, without establishing norms, learners will communicate through back channels (e.g., private chat, texting, Facebook). Norms in simultaneous learning will evolve, for better or worse.

Norms govern how Roomies and Zoomies interact with one another and delineate what will be tolerated and what will not. The behavior of each group is shaped in part by what the group expects of each other, whether it is a gathering of supplies, ways of giving and receiving feedback, or dividing up responsibilities for a task. The norms of the classroom are the beliefs and values we want the collective classroom—Roomies, Zoomies, and us—to abide by in simultaneous learning. These norms become a handy tool to refer to as learners transition to different contexts in simultaneous learning (see Figure 4.1).

4.1 PEER-TO-PEER LEARNING NORMS

- Give your Zoomies time to respond and share their thinking.
- Be adaptable to your learning and the learning of others.
- Ensure both your Roomies and Zoomies are ready to learn.
- Embrace that learning is challenging, and we will work together to be successful.
- Help each other find the necessary resources for learning.
- Understand that learning is a process that requires patience with self and others.
- Make a copy of the chat transcript and provide this to the class after each session.
- Chat is only used for classroom-related topics or socialization at appropriate times.

LINK NORMS TO CLASS AGREEMENTS

The norms we create in the simultaneous learning environment become the foundation for the agreements you want to use as we move forward in learning. These agreements are an essential component for an environment conducive to that learning. Well-crafted agreements communicate the expectations for the class and enhance the overall climate and student learning growth. However, there is one important aspect of establishing norms that we overlook in simultaneous learning: Norms must be explicitly taught. With Roomies and Zoomies, we cannot assume they know how to interact and engage in either synchronous or face-to-face learning. For example, two studies of efficient elementary and middle school classrooms found that in all cases the teachers taught the rules daily during the first week of school using discussion, modeling, and demonstrations (Emmer et al., 1980; Evertson & Emmer, 1982). New technologies further increase the need for rules in digital environments. The use of discussion boards and online collaborative tools has increased the need to ensure that students are taught the norms and expectations of how they work together (Staarman, 2009).

To be clear, these are agreements and not rules. Given the physical separation of Roomies and Zoomies, we must take every opportunity to forge a cohesive classroom community. Agreements represent the social contract of the classroom community, rather than a narrower set of behavioral guidelines that have been written by the teacher alone. A review of fifteen studies on the characteristics of these agreements confirmed what many teachers already know (Alter & Haydon, 2017):

➡ **A fewer number, rather than more, works better.** The recommendation is about three to five.

➡ **Co-construct them with students.** That's why we call them agreements. Even young students have a good sense of what is right and fair.

➡️ **State them positively.** Beware of a list of agreements that all begin with the word *No* because these do not tell students what they should do, only what they should not. Behavior cannot exist in a vacuum, and in the absence of clear statements students are left to speculate about what is acceptable in their breakout rooms and collaborative learning groups.

➡️ **Make them specific in nature.** Agreements that are specific in nature state explicitly what the expected behaviors for both Roomies and Zoomies should be, which is a key to building students' ability to self-regulate when they transition to asynchronous learning.

➡️ **Post the agreements.** Once developed, they should be clearly posted in your classroom (e.g., on the wall and on our learning management system). One way to do so is to put them on a chart that is behind your head so that students can see them in the room and while at a distance.

➡️ **Teach and rehearse the expectations.** This is a critical component for ensuring an efficient simultaneous learning environment. The agreements should be taught often during the initial transition to simultaneous learning and occasionally revisited throughout the remainder of the year, especially after school breaks or changes in the schedule (e.g., fully at a distance for a brief period of time). We should model each rule so that students can learn what they look and sound like. For example, if one of the agreements is about written communication on discussion boards, model examples of how these are done in ways that are respectful and academically appropriate.

CAN YOU IMAGINE TEACHING A FACE-TO-FACE CLASS WHERE EVERYONE HAD A BLANKET OVER THEIR HEADS?

Simultaneous learning poses some unique challenges when compared to face-to-face teaching. One expectation we have to confront early on in simultaneous learning is the issue of cameras with Zoomies. Some students turn them on; some do not. This initially seemed like a no-brainer—of course they should have them on! After all, could you even imagine teaching in a face-to-face class where everyone had a blanket over their heads? To be sure, we rely on being able to read students' facial expressions and body language so that we can teach responsively. But the issue of laptop cameras is more complicated. For instance, about 20 percent of our students are Muslim, and girls and women don't wear the hijab in their own homes. In households that are short on space, asking female family members to cover during their children's online learning seems burdensome. There are also students who don't want to show their homes to others for any number of reasons. Some students are self-conscious and do not want to look at themselves on camera for hours. There are also instances of students taking pictures of peers and then posting them on social media, poking fun through memes and such. These are sensitive topics that require sensitive approaches. One approach is to ask students to either turn on their camera or use their school picture so that they are easily recognizable to others. They can also turn their cameras on and point them to the ceiling so that they can show their work when requested. And when they are in breakout rooms, most of the Zoomies turn their cameras on so that they can see other Roomies and Zoomies.

The expectations for synchronous learning vary from one locale to the next, and we encourage you to consult with your district's requirements. Some schools that require school uniforms for face-to-face instruction continue to require them for Zoomies.

Certainly, it seems that school dress codes should remain in force, in the same way that behavioral ones do. We have also added other possible expectations to use with students when it comes to synchronous learning.

FOR YOUR CONSIDERATION

How will your Zoomies learn about the synchronous learning in your classroom? Here are some suggested items to address specific questions students are likely to have.

Getting Ready to Be a Zoomie

- Wear headphones if possible.
- Make sure you have completed the pre-class preparation activity so that you'll be ready to learn!
- Think about your goals for learning today. What do you want to achieve?
- Work with your family to find a quiet space that won't disturb other people in your house and won't distract you from learning.
- Prepare your learning space. Make sure you have a clear workspace to write and store your materials.
- If there are items that have personal information you wouldn't want other people to see, move them out of camera range.
- Check your lighting so that your classmates can see you.
- Check to see that your first and last names are on the screen.

Engaging in Class as a Zoomie

- Ask clarifying questions so you fully understand the learning intentions and success criteria for the lesson.
- Listen carefully to others and ask good questions!
- Use the reaction buttons to let your classmates know when you agree or disagree and give them a thumbs-up or a round of applause to encourage them.
- The hand-raising button helps all of us know when you've got something important to say.
- When you are not speaking, mute your microphone. It helps other people hear.
- Turn off notifications from email and social media so you aren't distracted.
- If you have a smartphone, shut it down so you aren't distracted.

Wrapping Up Class as a Zoomie

- Review the goals you set for today. Did you achieve them?
- Ask clarifying questions so you fully understand the learning intentions and success criteria for the lesson. Did you achieve the learning intentions and success criteria? How do you know?
- Make sure you know how to access assigned learning tasks to prepare for the next meeting.

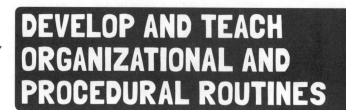

DEVELOP AND TEACH ORGANIZATIONAL AND PROCEDURAL ROUTINES

Another key component in initiating simultaneous learning involves the procedures and organizational structures needed to ensure learning takes place for both your synchronous learners and your face-to-face students. Although the environment may be different, many of the same organizational requirements remain the same. Provide a level of consistency with all digital resources. Have students access learning material in the same location. A one-stop-shop digital learning space minimizes confusion on where assignments and classroom resources are located.

1. **Provide weekly and monthly schedules so families and students can organize resources.** Chances are good that there is more than one school-age child in the household. Juggling the online schedules of multiple children can be challenging for even the most organized caregivers. Posting these schedules allows families and students to organize their time.

   - Build weekly and monthly schedules and show students where to find them on your LMS.

   - There may be protocols already developed by your district for designing your website, which is helpful to families as they don't need to learn how four different teachers organize in four idiosyncratic ways.

2. **Furnish a daily schedule at the beginning of the class meeting.** Learning intentions and success criteria are crucial for learning, and we must share what we discussed in Chapter 1 at each class meeting. Providing a schedule for the class meeting assists students in self-regulation of their cognitive and attentional resources.

   - The schedule should list the major learning events of the day in chronological order and may also include times.

   - The consistent use of a posted schedule establishes a predictable learning environment and assists learners in pacing their rate of work.

   - A daily schedule is particularly useful for students who have difficulty transitioning from one task to another and especially for younger children.

   - Posted daily schedules are an excellent support for some students with disabilities who may require more structure.

   - Students who are new to English can benefit from schedules that are paired with pictures.

3. **Use a staggered starting time for Roomies and Zoomies.**

- If the school day begins at 8:15 a.m., let Roomies arrive at school, gather their materials for the day, and prepare their learning space for the day.

- Conduct an abbreviated morning meeting with them to check in with them and get them started on their opening learning experience or task.

- Then start the day with the Zoomies. For example, this may be at 8:30 a.m.

- Conduct an abbreviated morning meeting with them to check in with them and get them started on their opening learning experience or task.

- Then engage both Roomies and Zoomies in a joint morning meeting and their simultaneous learning day.

4. **Teach students the signals you will use.** Teachers need a signal to gain the attention of students at the beginning of class, when students are engaged in dialogue with peers, or when transitioning from one activity to another.

- The signals should be taught daily at the start of simultaneous learning and reinforced frequently until students respond quickly and consistently.

- The use of a signal to gain attention promotes student engagement by minimizing the amount of lost instructional time.

  This fourth point deserves further attention. A study of first-grade classrooms found that teachers who spent time orienting students to the next activity required less time for the transition, and the students in these classrooms spent more time in child-directed learning activities such as collaborative learning than those in classrooms that did not use transition techniques (Cameron et al., 2005).

- Smooth transitions minimize the behavioral difficulties that can arise.

- Students with behavioral disabilities are especially vulnerable to loosely managed transitions. In many cases, they are blamed for the problem behavior, without consideration for the lack of environmental signals that could have prevented the difficulty from arising in the first place.

- Students who are new to English are also vulnerable to a lack of signals. When directions are only provided verbally and are not paired with audible or gestural signals, they may miss the language-based directions and be unfairly viewed as being noncompliant.

- Use an online elapsed timer display when setting up tasks students will be completing in real time. This further signals to students how to best use their remaining time to complete independent work such as reflective writing.

- Many distance learning platforms feature elapsed timers for small group breakout rooms. Make sure students are aware of these features so that they can monitor their use of time in peer-to-peer small group learning.

5. **Create procedures for how students will gather materials and resources.** Few things are more frustrating than trying to figure out where to find materials for learning.

   - Clearly label digital folders by date and topic so that students can easily locate them.

   - Ask Roomies and Zoomies to access digital resources so that they are looking at and using the same materials and resources.

6. **Create procedures for how students will submit assignments**. Over the course of the school year, students will turn in a large number of assignments. Invariably, some of these documents will lack important information such as a name or date. Grading is further complicated when the topic of the assignment is unclear. With the advent of digital resources, the naming of documents holds similar problems. It is difficult to process and locate a hundred assignments that are all unhelpfully named "Math Assignment."

   - Teach students a system for heading their assignments at the beginning of the year to make recordkeeping easier.

   - Be sure to instruct them on properly naming the file so that you (and they) can locate it quickly. The title of the document should contain the student's last name, the name of the course, and a one- or two-word description.

Simultaneous learning is the combination of distance learning and face-to-face learning in the same learning experience. The implementation of simultaneous learning must not result in an additive approach to designing and implementing rigorous and engaging experiences that move learning forward. Thus, establishing norms, procedures, and processes for this type of learning environment provides the structures that allow us to extract and implement what works best from both distance learning and face-to-face learning environments. What this now allows us to do is focus more on creating rigorous and engaging learning experiences and tasks—the focus of the next chapter.

5 ENGAGEMENT IN SIMULTANEOUS LEARNING

In this section:

- ☐ WHAT IS MEANT BY *ENGAGEMENT*?
- ☐ A NEW WAY OF THINKING ABOUT ENGAGEMENT
- ☐ MOTIVATION AND TASK DESIGN
- ☐ DESIGN A SCHEDULE TO PROMOTE ENGAGEMENT
- ☐ CHALLENGING, BUT POSSIBLE AND POTENTIALLY REWARDING

When it comes to student learning, the primary finding is this: *Student time spent engaged in relevant content appears to be an essential variable for which there is no substitute* (Rosenshine & Berliner, 1978, p. 12). Yet, this is a real challenge in simultaneous learning for many of the reasons we have hinted at in the previous chapters. For Ms. Lewanowicz, Ms. Marquez, and the teachers of Sanchez ISD, fostering, nurturing, and sustaining engagement is a daily challenge. Looking first at distance learning, we consider that there are multiple variables that can and do influence the level of engagement and persistence in what we want them to learn. For example,

➡ Do our learners have access to a stable and reliable internet connection?

➡ Do they have the necessary technology to access our distance learning classroom and required materials (e.g., digital tools, textbooks)?

➡ What distractions are in their learning environment?

For learners in our classrooms, we also have to ensure they have access to the necessary materials and manage the distractions. What differs between these two groups of students is that we have the benefit of immediacy in a face-to-face setting. Walking a glue stick or graphic organizer over to a Roomie that does not have their supplies is not a luxury we have with our Zoomies. Likewise, when two Roomies are distracting each other during a mathematic lesson (e.g., using the manipulatives for something other than solving the problem), we simply address it on the spot. However, if Zoomies will not turn on their cameras, unmute their microphones, or even log in to class, engagement in relevant content is not just a challenge but a problem. This is one of the striking differences between face-to-face and distance learning. Together, in simultaneous learning, this is more apparent than ever. So, what are we to do?

WE MUST DIRECT THE BULK OF OUR ENERGY TO ENSURE THAT OUR SIMULTANEOUS LEARNERS HAVE RIGOROUS AND ENGAGING TASKS WHEN THEY ARE WITH US OR LOGGED INTO CLASS.

Let's take a step back a minute and first direct our energies toward something we, as teachers, have immediate control over: the nature of our learning experiences and tasks related to what Rosenshine and Berliner (1978) refer to as relevant content. While working alongside our instructional leaders, school social workers, school counselors, and parent/guardian advocacy groups, we should strive to get the necessary technology and support in the hands of our learners. However, we must direct the bulk of our energy to ensure that our simultaneous learners have rigorous and engaging tasks when they are with us or logged into class. What we have discovered is that in simultaneous learning the fostering, nurturing, and sustaining of engagement is the same for our face-to-face learners as it is for our distance learners. Again, we do not have to double our efforts but adapt the learning experiences and tasks that we design to be compatible in both environments.

Notice that the three bulleted items above only addressed the "nuts and bolts" of learners engaging at a distance in simultaneous learning. The list did not move beyond the logistics, paying no attention to the actual learning experience and tasks. That is the main idea of this chapter: In simultaneous learning, fostering, nurturing, and sustaining student engagement in the most relevant content, skills, and understandings is the same for our face-to-face learners as it is for those learning from a distance.

WHAT IS MEANT BY *ENGAGEMENT?*

We do not believe that we are alone in stating that student engagement is one of those ideas that is very difficult to define, but we know it when we see it. For the purposes of teaching and learning in a simultaneous learning environment, recognizing what is and is not engagement will suffice. Let's look at a specific example. A student sitting at their desk staring out the window could easily be pegged as a disengaged student—well, disengaged in what we have identified as relevant content. They clearly are engaged in whatever is happening outside or in their mind. This is where we have to be very careful in our assumptions. This learner may actually be thinking about their experiences and the experiences of the main character, Starr Carter, in the 2017 novel *The Hate U Give*. Similarly, a learner may have their video off and microphone muted because they are simply logged on and then off to play video games. This student may also simply want to avoid you and their peers seeing what their home looks like. Our point is this—defining and recognizing student engagement in simultaneous learning as a single concept is hard, maybe impossible.

So, to navigate simultaneous learning, we must think about student engagement, not as a single concept but as a multidimensional event. One way to explain the multidimensional nature of engagement is to look at student engagement as the combination of emotion, behavior, and cognition. Whether face-to-face or from a distance, students potentially engage in learning in three ways that include their

1. Personal feelings about the content, material, and learning task

2. Behaviors or actions while in the classroom or logged in to Zoom

3. Thinking while engaging in the learning experience or task

Student engagement can be considered across a few dimensions:

1. **Emotional engagement:** how the student feels

2. **Behavioral engagement:** the behaviors or actions of the student

3. **Cognitive engagement:** what the student is thinking

How we as teachers set up our face-to-face and virtual classrooms has a major influence on both the type and level of engagement of the students on a daily basis. Too much emphasis on behavioral engagement (e.g., rules, procedures) and learners won't like being in the classroom or on Zoom (emotional) and will think about other things when they are supposed to be engaging in the learning associated with the learning intentions and success criteria (cognitive). Turning all attention to cognitive engagement, consider that behavioral disengagement ensues and learners once again don't like being in the classroom. In simultaneous learning, this is commonly seen in Zoom fatigue, where our Zoomies spend six hours logged in to class. For our Roomies, this comes from trying to squeeze an entire curriculum into two days of face-to-face learning (e.g., A–B model and split day model). Finally, while high levels of emotional

> WHEN LEARNERS ARE A COLLECTION OF RECTANGLES ON A SCREEN, HOW DO WE NOTICE, MAKE SENSE OF, AND RESPOND TO THESE THREE WAYS OF THINKING ABOUT ENGAGING?

engagement lead to great fun, the fun can lead to chaos and limited thinking. Furthermore, when learners are a collection of rectangles on a screen, how do we notice, make sense of, and then respond to these three ways of thinking about engaging?

A NEW WAY OF THINKING ABOUT ENGAGEMENT

OUR FOCUS MUST SHIFT BEYOND WHETHER OR NOT THE STUDENTS COMPLETED THE TASK, LOGGED ON TO ZOOM, OR LOOK LIKE THEY ARE PAYING ATTENTION.

Working with Roomies, or any face-to-face interaction with learners, allows us to "read the room" and make immediate adjustments about what to do next. Standing within six feet of a student in Ms. Marquez's classroom or joining Ms. Lewanowicz on the carpet gives us access to real-time data that is not as easily accessible when those learners are logging in through Zoom. At Sanchez ISD, they must adopt a different way of thinking about engagement beyond emotional, behavioral, and cognitive. Amy Berry (2020) interviewed teachers about the conception of engagement, and most often they saw engagement more in terms of their observable outcomes. In simultaneous learning, our focus must shift beyond whether or not the students completed the task, logged on to Zoom, or look like they are paying attention. In simultaneous learning, we need more than participating, and we may not have access to real-time data about emotional and cognitive data. Of course, we can have observable cues of students engaging in doing tasks. Berry called this *participating* but noted in her survey that many teachers wanted more. This led to her model with three forms of engagement and three of disengagement (see Figure 5.1). According to Berry, students can move between these forms. Naturally, we all want to help students move from participating or "doing" to investing and driving their own learning.

5.1 A NEW MODEL FOR THINKING ABOUT LEARNER ENGAGEMENT

ACTIVE ← —————————————————— PASSIVE —————————————————— → ACTIVE

Disrupting	Avoiding	Withdrawing	Participating	Investing	Driving
Distracting others Disrupting the learning	Looking for ways to avoid work Off-task behavior	Being distracted Physically separating from group	Doing work Paying attention Responding to questions	Asking questions Valuing the learning	Setting goals Seeking feedback Self-assessment

DISENGAGEMENT	ENGAGEMENT

Source: Berry, A. (2020). Disrupting to driving: Exploring upper primary teachers' perspectives on student engagement. *Teachers and Teaching, 26*(2), 145–165. doi:10.1080/13540602.2020.1757421

Therefore, the experiences and tasks that we design and implement in simultaneous learning should motivate and scaffold both Zoomies and Roomies in their journey to investing and driving their own learning. We have had a lot of success using the continuum of engagement to have conversations with students about what each level looks like in this specific class. Students can record their ideas on a shared document and be asked to reflect on their level of engagement following a class session. Some teachers provide time for students to do this daily or weekly, asking students for evidence to support their self-assessment. Every time we change the format of school, we should revisit the engagement continuum and invite students to name actions and behaviors that would be considered in this format of school.

MOTIVATION AND TASK DESIGN

How a student perceives a learning experience or task strongly influences the degree to which they engage (e.g., active disengagement, passive disengagement, passive engagement, active engagement). For example, whether face-to-face or at a distance, a learner will make an internal assessment about the relative usefulness of a particular experience or task. This, in turn, influences their willingness to raise a hand or use the chat feature to seek help, to exert effort in the breakout rooms, and to manage their feelings of anxiety about completing the task. In simultaneous learning, motivating students to engage and persist in our learning experience or task can be based on four components of the perceived value of the learning experience or task by students (Eccles, 2005):

> WHETHER FACE-TO-FACE OR AT A DISTANCE, A LEARNER WILL MAKE AN INTERNAL ASSESSMENT ABOUT THE RELATIVE USEFULNESS OF A PARTICULAR EXPERIENCE OR TASK.

1. **Interest.** This refers to the level of enjoyment a student has or gets from engaging in and persisting through the experience or task. How do you design tasks so that they tap into student interests? In what ways can you place core experience and task into a context that would appeal to your learners (e.g., narrative writing is undertaken through the eyes of a journalist, a book talk is done as a literary critic, exponential growth is modeled using the role of an epidemiologist)?

2. **Utility value.** Students have short-term and long-term goals. How can we leverage this through our learning experiences and tasks? For example, we can use the information we gain about our learners to not only build strong, positive student–teacher relationships but also to help them find utility value in what they do in both face-to-face and distance learning.

3. **Attainment value.** We can enhance the attainment value by incorporating student goals into our simultaneous learning. We will look at examples of this in later chapters. Given the role of asynchronous learning in almost all models of simultaneous learning, explicitly teaching goal setting in reading, mathematics, or any other content area magnifies task value by linking the task to one's sense of self and either personal or social identity.

4. **Cost.** Finally, learners internally evaluate what may be given up by choosing to engage in a specific learning experience or task. For example, logging off of their online gaming platform to join your trigonometry class is a real dilemma. Furthermore, how do we ensure that their time logged in to class or in our classroom does not have any negative experiences associated with it? For example, requiring them to turn their cameras on may jeopardize their emotional safety and make the cost of this task too high.

Here are suggestions for ensuring that your task design is inclusive—engaging **all** learners in your simultaneous learning environment.

Videos

- Use closed captions for your presentations and videos.

- Offer copies of the transcripts of the chat boxes to all learners. These can be posted on your learning management system (LMS) to reduce the need for paper.

- Make videos readily accessible if possible so they can be watched again for those who may benefit from experiencing content more than once.

Images

- Aim for representation in your use of images and videos. One way to enhance task value and a sense of inclusion is to make sure learners can "see themselves" in your images and videos.

- Ensure the color and font on your slides, the writing utensil you use with the document camera, and the lighting allow learners to comfortably see the images.

- When learners are expected to view the image and take in essential information, do not talk or provide audio while they are observing the image. Give them time to just look at the image.

- Provide digital copies of the images on your LMS so that learners can revisit them during their asynchronous time or pull them up on their own devices.

Printed Materials

- Use readable PDFs, not scans of texts. You can check the readability of a PDF by trying to copy and paste individual words. If you can do that, a screen reader will be able to detect text; otherwise, the screen reader will simply interpret it as an image.

- Clearly define special terms or jargon to help support and build toward understanding for multilingual constituents for whom English may not be a native language.

- Provide electronic versions of any printed material.

Face-to-Face Experiences and Tasks

- Ensure that emotional safety is secured before engaging learners in social interaction. Initially, vary activities so that Roomies and Zoomies have the option to not just partner or engage in collaborative/cooperative learning, but rather have time for individual work.

- Preassign groups to ensure the individual dynamics of the group or team are conducive to learning (see Fisher, Frey, & Almarode, 2021).

- Establish and model norms for experiences and tasks that require a great deal of social interaction. Provide channels for all simultaneous learners to communicate with you and share feedback about their experiences in a confidential way.

Although the research on student perceptions of task value is interesting, translating those four components of task value into practice is another thing altogether. Are there guidelines, suggestions, or even specific strategies that might help us enhance student interest, utility value, and attainment value and lower the cost of engaging and persisting in simultaneous learning? Fortunately, there is research on what this might look like in practice. In 2015, Antonetti and Garver published *17,000 Classroom Visits Can't Be Wrong,* where they reported on data from over 17,000 classroom walk-throughs. Today, this database contains more than 23,000 walk-throughs, some of which are virtual walk-throughs. Embedded in the data were eight features of classroom tasks that were associated with sustained engagement. As learners fluctuate in their levels of engagement, we can make adjustments in these eight areas to re-engage those learners that have waned in their engagement, as well as sustain the engagement of other learners before they disengage.

➡️ **Make sure there are clear and modeled expectations**. Does the learner have a clear understanding of what success looks like? This characteristic refers to clear learning intentions and success criteria. Recall the examples shared in Figures 1.1 and 1.2. How do we differentiate the learning intentions and success criteria for simultaneous learning?

➡️ **Provide more opportunities for personal response**. Does the student have the opportunity to bring their own personal experiences to the learning experience? Examples include any strategy or learning experience that invites learners to bring their own background, interests, or expertise to the conversation. Zoomies can **safely**, and **when appropriate**, use their living environment as their learning environment.

➡️ **Create a sense of audience**. Does the learner have a sense that this experience or task matters to someone other than the teacher, the grade book, or merely clicking the submit button on Canvas? Tasks that have a sense of audience are those tasks that mean something to individuals beyond the teacher. In simultaneous learning, Roomies can serve as an audience for Zoomies as they teach something back to their peers.

Similarly, Zoomies can serve as the audience for Roomies as they narrate a recording comparing and contrasting student work samples (see Figure 1.6).

➡ **Increase the levels of social interaction.** Does the learner have opportunities to socially interact with peers in breakout rooms or through discussion boards? Providing learners with opportunities to talk about their learning and interact with their peers supports their meaning making and development of conceptual understanding. Are there ways to structure simultaneous learning so that Roomies can interact with Zoomies?

➡ **Ensure emotional safety.** Does the learner feel safe in asking questions or making mistakes? To be blunt, if learners feel threatened in your classroom, they will not engage. What steps are we taking to make sure our learners feel respected, valued, and cared for beyond an attendance record?

➡ **Offer more choice.** Does the learner have choices in how they access the learning? As learners engage in any learning experience or task, we should offer choices around who they work with, what materials and manipulatives are available, and what learning strategies they can use to engage in the experience and complete the task. In simultaneous learning, do we provide an online portal or common location for materials and manipulatives?

➡ **Utilize novelty.** Does the learner experience the learning from a new or unique perspective? Learners do not pay attention to boring things. How can we present content in a way that captures their attention?

➡ **Make the learning authentic.** Does the learner experience an authentic learning experience, or is the experience sterile and unrealistic (e.g., a worksheet versus problem-solving scenario; simply converting a PPT to a narrated slide deck versus using reciprocal teaching to gather and share information)?

As each of us strives to foster, nurture, and sustain student engagement in a simultaneous learning environment, we have to keep several main points in mind:

1. Engaging learners in a face-to-face environment utilizes the same principles as engaging them from a distance.

2. Engagement is a multidimensional idea that is best described on a continuum from active disengagement to active engagement with passivity in between the two.

3. To sustain engagement, we have to constantly monitor and be prepared to adjust simultaneous learning when engagement and persistence wane in our learners.

DESIGN A SCHEDULE TO PROMOTE ENGAGEMENT

Simultaneous learning requires that we constantly monitor and be prepared to adjust simultaneous learning when engagement and persistence wane in our learners. In addition, the different models, all of which combine face-to-face and distance learning, require us to constantly monitor the time variable. How we allot and allocate instructional time in simultaneous learning can and will have an influence on engagement and persistence. Let's return back to the nuts and bolts of engagement and the role they play in promoting engagement.

Earlier in this chapter, we mentioned the idea of Zoom fatigue. Teachers and students have experienced the "Zoom exhaustion" that comes from too many hours trying to sit still and remain engaged in front of a screen. Likewise, face-to-face days should not be used to cram everything from a particular standard into two days. While we may find that replicating the school schedule during simultaneous learning days to be the easiest approach, this is not workable for teacher or students. Five or six hours of daily instruction, complete with the same bell schedules, recess breaks, and lunch schedules, is too difficult for sustained engagement. Eventually, this will even lead to the "Sunday evening blues"—anxiety about tomorrow's school day begins to build on Sunday evening. Specifically, for our Zoomies, their homes, apartments, the Boys and Girls Club, and the local YMCA do not run on a school schedule.

Maximizing the engagement of our simultaneous learners means that we return to our discussion about clarity for learning. How is our time best spent during face-to-face learning, synchronous learning, and asynchronous learning? Integrating the lessons learned from the research on task value (Eccles, 2005) and classroom walk-throughs (Antonetti & Garver, 2015), the time we are with students, face-to-face and synchronous, should be prioritized for connection, discussion, and interaction. The time that learners must devote to asynchronous learning may be best used for deliberate practice, building background knowledge, processing, and self-reflecting. When designing and implementing rigorous and engaging experiences that move learning forward, think about the what, why, and how of the learning (i.e., clarity) and then the nature of the experiences in each context.

HOW IS OUR TIME BEST SPENT DURING FACE-TO-FACE LEARNING, SYNCHRONOUS LEARNING, AND ASYNCHRONOUS LEARNING?

Within each model for simultaneous learning, consistency and predictability of the schedule will help maximize engagement. When we talked about novelty in promoting student engagement, that novelty referred to the learning experience or the task, not the schedule. In simultaneous learning, teachers, students, and families must know who is where on what day and when they have to be there. This ensures the consistency and predictability needed for the continuity of learning. We must work with our colleagues to design weekly schedules for A–B groups. Then, we must ensure that how we communicate clarity and expectations for learning experiences and tasks is shared early and adhered to so that when learners transition between face-to-face and distance learning, they are comfortable and confident about what is to be accomplished before, during, and after each learning experience. As we noted previously, this includes consistency and predictability in sharing learning intentions, success criteria, and any assessments so that students have a clear sense of purpose and can ask questions in advance (e.g., face-to-face, using the chat feature, or discussion boards).

A scheduling template or grade-level or schoolwide master schedule for the particular simultaneous learning model can help tremendously in providing students with consistent and predictable ways to engage with the content, with you, and with their peers. A grade-level or schoolwide master schedule is particularly useful for families with several children attending a school, and at the secondary level for students who are meeting with several subject matter teachers. Where learners are and when they are there will provide the structural and relational supports that promote engagement. We have observed countless situations where confusion about where to be and when defaults to simply not logging in at all—disengagement.

DISENGAGEMENT MAY BE A SIDE EFFECT OF CONFLICTING SCHEDULES.

Along those same lines, disengagement may be a side effect of conflicting schedules. In simultaneous learning, we may be doing our very best to schedule sessions that meet the needs of our learners. However, without a grade-level or schoolwide master schedule, students and their families may be juggling sessions and meetings that change each day. What is a student supposed to do when the English teacher and a special education support person are unknowingly asking for the same time?

The nuts and bolts matter. If we devote significant time during our planning days (e.g., A–B model and full week model) and planning periods (e.g., split day model) to design and implement rigorous and engaging learning experiences, but then create a schedule that is not managed by anyone, we subvert our work to foster, nurture, and sustain engagement.

CHALLENGING, BUT POSSIBLE AND POTENTIALLY REWARDING

As we transition to a closer look at the specific elements of asynchronous and synchronous learning experiences and tasks, we want to recall an earlier conversation about the relationship between teaching and learning and tools for teaching and learning (see Figure 5.2).

5.2 FUNCTIONS AND TOOLS

Teacher wants students to	Student Engagement Opportunities	Sample Digital Resources
Find Information	• Can locate information sources • Can organize and analyze information sources for accuracy and utility to the task • Locating information is driven by curiosity and topic	• Wakelet • Google/Google Scholar • Quizlet • Pear Deck • eBooks
Use Information	• Can cite sources of information • Makes judgments about how best to use information • Asks questions the information provokes	• Evernote • OneNote • Flipgrid • Grammarly • PlayPosit • TurnItIn • Nearpod • Didax Math Manipulatives • Toytheater Virtual Manipulatives • Boomwriter
Create Information	• Can write and discuss information according to grade-level expectations • Transforms information in order to explore ideas new to the learner • Takes academic risks to innovate	• GSuite for Education • Office 365 • ThingLink • iMovie • Padlet • Seesaw • Screencastify • Google Drawings • Jamboard • StoryboardThat
Share Information	• Accurately matches purpose to audience • Uses metacognitive thinking to identify the best strategies for the stated purpose • Is resourceful and resilient	• Animoto • Storybird • WeVideo • Jamboard • YouTube

Source: Adapted from Fisher, D., Frey, N., & Hattie, J. (2020). *The distance learning playbook, grades K–12: Teaching for engagement and impact in any setting.* Corwin.

In education, we have so many options for resources and tools that are available to support our teaching and student learning in simultaneous environments. Selecting your suite of tools for Roomies and Zoomies can be challenging, as there are so many to choose from. The endless lists of tools and resources can be daunting to scroll through. These lists do not provide guidance or information based on the particular simultaneous learning model or the local context of your school, classroom, and learners. To ensure that designing and implementing rigorous and engaging experiences that move learning forward is possible, even if stressful, here are some reflective questions that can help us make decisions on which tools from Figure 5.2 make the most sense for your model, school, classroom, and learners:

➡ What learning function does this tool fulfill?

➡ Is it developmentally appropriate for my students to use with minimal adult assistance?

➡ Does this tool have accessibility features that are aligned to digital compliance requirements (e.g., provides closed captioning, supports screen reader software)? What are they?

6 ACCELERATING LEARNING

In this section:

- ☐ FEATURES OF ACCELERATION
  1. IDENTIFY SKILLS AND CONCEPTS THAT HAVE YET TO BE LEARNED.
  2. PROVIDE KEY ASPECTS OF KNOWLEDGE IN ADVANCE OF INSTRUCTION.
  3. INCREASE THE RELEVANCE OF STUDENTS' LEARNING.
  4. CREATE ACTIVE, FAST-PACED LEARNING EXPERIENCES.
  5. BUILD STUDENTS' CONFIDENCE.

Learning loss. The COVID slide. The gap year. We've all heard the predictions that students will fail to learn as a result of distance, remote, hybrid, simultaneous, hyflex, and blended learning. There are students whose performance or understanding has been compromised. Yet there are other students who performed well, even better than in their past. The predictions of learning loss, such as the "COVID slide" projected by the Annenberg Institute at Brown University (Kuhfeld et al., 2020a) of 32 percent to 37 percent in reading and 50 percent to 63 percent in mathematics, have been challenged by large-scale data presented by groups such as NWEA and their 4.4 million MAP assessments of Grades 3 to 8 that show relatively little loss for those who took the assessment (Kuhfeld et al., 2020b). But there is solemn news within those findings. Up to 25 percent of the students who took the test in 2019 did not do so in 2020. Many of those students were from low-income households, often Black or Latinx. While some students did well, others fell further behind. In many school systems, existing equity gaps further widened. The distribution of learning, and learning loss, has not been even across all groups of learners (i.e., race, ethnicity, and socioeconomic status). Even pre-pandemic, it never was.

If we really think about it, the phrase *learning loss* is mostly wrong. Learning loss implies that they once had it and now they do not have specific learning. It is hard to find evidence that students forgot what they had learned in the past. The reality is that some students experienced less than ideal instruction and did not learn all that they could have in a particular content area or grade level. And yet, some students learned more than they would have in that same content area or grade level.

Perhaps we need to think about unrealized potential. What could students have learned? Where would their learning be if there had not been a pandemic? But let's be careful of engaging in too much deficit thinking. There are some pretty impressive things that students did learn during their time in distance learning. Who would have thought that second graders would be logging into video conferences, problem-solving technology glitches, and collaborating with peers in breakout rooms? Who could have predicted that high schoolers would design their own learning projects, complete science labs in their homes, and develop personal fitness plans with the physical education instructor? When we spend too much time focused on deficits and the gaps that may have occurred, we run the risk of lowering our expectations for all students. We might begin to think that students could not possibly achieve this year because of what happened in the past year. However, let us be clear, we are not in denial about the realities that students have faced during the abrupt transition to distance learning. What we aim to do is draw attention to the potential that focusing on the gaps and the loss will result in remediation programs and lowered expectations for students for years to come. Our learners do not need that! Students need us to believe that they can learn and then design and implement rigorous and engaging experiences that communicate those expectations to them. Instead of learning loss and unrealized potentials, let us focus on learning leaps. Specifically, we need to focus on acceleration and learning recovery.

Drawing on the research regarding acceleration for students identified as gifted and talented, the effect size of acceleration is 0.68 (www.visiblelearningmetax.com), well worth the effort to change the narrative. Acceleration does not mean skipping a grade level or covering two chapters in five minutes. Acceleration and learning recovery do not mean that students should repeat the grade, which is being recommended in some state legislatures as we write. In fact, grade-level retention is one of the most negative influences on learning in the Visible Learning database (www.visiblelearningmetax.com). Instead, acceleration and learning recovery means focusing on and ensuring that the core and key parts of the curriculum are covered and that they are covered with depth. Of course, the narrative of acceleration needs to be supported with high-quality learning experiences that have an impact. The fact is that teachers like Ms. Lewanowicz, Ms. Marquez, and those from Sanchez ISD are very good at achieving the expectations that they have for students, high or low.

In terms of the evidence on acceleration, we'll explore five areas that are important in creating these types of experiences for students.

1. **Identify skills and concepts that have yet to be learned.**
   - What tools do we have to notice what students still need to learn?
   - How can we ensure that we do not focus instructional time on content students have already learned?

2. **Provide key aspects of knowledge in advance of instruction.**
   - How can we use what we have learned about asynchronous learning to build background knowledge and vocabulary?
   - What content can be previewed before synchronous learning time?

3. **Increase the relevance of students' learning.**
   - How can we capture students' attention and interest and ensure that they see the value in the things that they are learning?
   - Can our students answer the question "Why am I learning this?"

4. **Create active, fast-paced learning experiences.**
   - Can we develop lessons that move quickly, perhaps cycling through information several times, and allow students to engage?
   - How can we ensure that students are active and practice as part of our lessons?

5. **Build students' confidence.**
   - Are the students building their confidence in their learning as that helps build competence?
   - What successes do students have that we can celebrate?
   - How can we learn to be strength-spotters rather than deficit-describers?

> GRADE-LEVEL RETENTION IS ONE OF THE MOST NEGATIVE INFLUENCES ON LEARNING IN THE VISIBLE LEARNING DATABASE.

> HOW CAN WE LEARN TO BE STRENGTH-SPOTTERS RATHER THAN DEFICIT-DESCRIBERS?

FEATURES OF ACCELERATION

1. **Identify skills and concepts that have yet to be learned.** As we noted in Chapter 1, analyzing the standards to identify skills and concepts is an important part of the teaching and learning process. In that first chapter, we focused on the development of learning intentions and success criteria, but the analysis of standards is much more important than that. When you understand the skills and concepts that students are expected to

master, you can identify which of these have yet to be learned. As Nuthall (2007) noted, about 40 percent of instruction minutes are spent on things that students already know. To accelerate learning, that number has to be much lower. Importantly, that 40 percent could differ from student to student. They all come to class knowing things. The problem is that some of them know this and others know that, so we tend to teach everything that anyone might need to learn. Obviously, that's not very effective and will not allow us to accelerate learning.

Assessments provide information about what students have yet to learn. These assessments can be informal or more formal. But you need the data if you are going to accelerate learning. Some samples of data collection that can be used to accelerate learning can be found in Figure 6.1. These are simply examples. Think about the data you have that will allow you to determine what students have already learned and what they still need to learn. And then use that information to design synchronous and asynchronous experiences that are tailored to the needs of your students. If you are able to redirect the 40 percent of instructional minutes away from things that students already know and allocate that time to things that they still need to know, you'll contribute to their learning leaps.

> **RESEARCH SUGGESTS THAT ABOUT 40% OF INSTRUCTION MINUTES ARE SPENT ON THINGS THAT STUDENTS ALREADY KNOW.**

6.1 DATA COLLECTION EXAMPLES

Tool	What You Can Learn	Example
Writing Sample	• Mechanics and conventions • Organization • Voice • Vocabulary and word choice	Students were asked to brainstorm ideas in response to a writing prompt during synchronous learning. Their teacher provided them voice-recorded feedback and they used that feedback to develop their response. The teacher noted that several students needed to work on spelling while others had no errors. Other students needed work on their organization and flow. And all students could benefit from additional academic vocabulary development.
Knowledge Inventory	• Background knowledge • Key vocabulary • Misconceptions	In advance of a unit of investigation in science, the students completed an inventory that included multiple-choice and constructed-response opportunities. The teacher noted that most students had significant background knowledge related to this content and did not exhibit common misconceptions. A few students needed work on academic vocabulary.
Retelling	• Organization • Ideas and content • Oral language	Students were asked to record, using Flipgrid, information about the previous math content. The teacher had modeled retelling and students knew how to explain their thinking. The teacher used these videos to identify areas of strength and areas that confused students.
Commercially Available Benchmark Assessment (e.g., iReady, MAPS, LevelSet)	• Progress toward specific standards	The school collects benchmark assessment data on a regular basis, and teachers use the information to identify areas of focus. They also use this information to ensure that lessons are not focused on skills students have already mastered.

Again, these are simply examples of the ways in which we can find and use information to accelerate learning. The goal is to focus instructional minutes on things that students have already learned. Importantly, we should focus on the strengths we see in the data and become "strength-spotters" so that we recognize that our students have, and are, learning.

2. **Provide key aspects of knowledge in advance of instruction.** This is the power and potential of asynchronous learning. And providing key aspects of knowledge in advance of instruction is a major tenant of flipped learning (e.g., Bergmann & Sams, 2012). One concern that many have expressed with simultaneous and hybrid forms of learning is the loss of instruction minutes. To address that issue and accelerate learning, it's important to focus on the preview aspect of synchronous learning that was discussed in Chapter 2.

More specifically, it's valuable to build background knowledge and ensure students understand the vocabulary that will be used during instruction. Background knowledge and vocabulary are significant predictors of understanding and comprehension. Much of learning is connecting the new with the known. Thus, if we can provide key aspects of knowledge in advance and build what students know, instructional time can focus on the new information.

Students can learn new vocabulary through interactive videos, as was described in Chapter 3. They can also complete vocabulary knowledge assessments and identify words that they still need to learn. Importantly, we should not return to the old "assign, define, test" approach to vocabulary in which students are assigned a bunch of words, told to look them up, and then tested on those words. Vocabulary learning is much more robust than that and requires repeated experiences with the words and opportunities to use the words. And by the way, we all learn a lot of words from reading and interacting with others.

There are two main ways to build background knowledge: direct experiences and indirect experiences. Direct approaches are those that allow the learner to experience the world around them. In the past, field trips, labs, and a range of other direct experiences were used to build background knowledge. Some of this can still occur in the physical classroom, but given the constraints of time, it's wise to build student experiences virtually and during asynchronous learning. There are a number of museums, for example, that provide access to their collection, and some include guided learning experiences. In addition, there are a number of virtual labs and experiments that students can do. Of course, teachers can also provide students with the tools they need to engage in the labs and simulations at home.

Indirect experiences, on the other hand, involve building background in surrogate ways. Indirect experiences can include teacher modeling, wide reading, graphic organizers, and guest speakers, to name a few. Wide reading is a particularly useful way to build background knowledge in an indirect way. In fact, wide reading is one of the cheapest and easiest ways for people to rapidly build their understanding, especially for students who struggle with reading. In the absence of direct experiences, wide reading is the most effective way for building background knowledge (Marzano, 2004). Our research and experience suggest that there are four things that must be in place to increase reading volume (see Figure 6.2).

WIDE READING IS ONE OF THE CHEAPEST AND EASIEST WAYS FOR PEOPLE TO RAPIDLY BUILD THEIR UNDERSTANDING, ESPECIALLY FOR STUDENTS WHO STRUGGLE WITH READING.

6.2 ABCDs OF RAISING READING VOLUME

Aspect	Explanation
Access	If there is little to read in your home, you're less likely to read. To raise the volume of reading, students must have access to texts. There have been a number of efforts to "flood" students with things to read, but a steady diet is probably a better approach. This means that books need to be going home with students and that students need access to books like they do to technology and the internet.
Book Talks and "Blessing Books"	When trusted others make recommendations about a text, potential readers are more likely to read it. To promote wide reading, students need recommendations from others. Book talks conducted by trusted adults and peers can spur voluntary reading.
Choice	When students have choice over their reading materials, they are more likely to read. Choice is key to motivation and academic independence. Students who have opportunities to choose their own books develop elaborate strategies for selecting books and are more likely to become intrinsically motivated readers.
Discussions About Texts	Readers need opportunities to talk about what they are reading with others. These can be blogs and other digital interactions, or they can be times that students interact synchronously. Book clubs and literature circles are especially useful, and students can schedule these to occur outside of class.

3. **Increase the relevance of students' learning.** When learning is relevant, students are more likely to allocate resources to learn. And by resources, we mean time and attention. We noted the value of relevance in the first chapter and the importance of motivation in the second. There was even a screenshot that included why students were learning the content. Here, we want to emphasize that accelerating learning requires that students believe that what they are learning is worth the effort.

The typical ways for increasing relevance include making connections beyond the walls of the classroom and providing students with opportunities to learn about themselves. For example, a teacher might note that this content will help them understand why it rains more in one place than another. Or the teacher might say that this is an opportunity to understand how you solve problems and how your skills in problem-solving differ from others. Generally, these still work to ensure that students find relevance in their learning.

But the reality is that this aspect of learning is often neglected or rushed. There are far too many students who have no idea how to answer the question, "Why am I learning this?" And there are a lot of us educators who aren't sure either. We need to seriously consider the reasons that students need to know or be able to do something and then explore that with students. When they accept the challenge of learning, and see that learning as relevant, they are much more likely to learn. And that's acceleration.

Before we leave the topic of relevance, we'd also like to note that your passion for students, their learning, and the content they are learning contributes to relevance. We can all remember a time that we learned something simply because the person teaching us was so excited. Bring that passion and excitement to your class and show

WHEN THEY ACCEPT THE CHALLENGE OF LEARNING, AND SEE THAT LEARNING AS RELEVANT, THEY ARE MUCH MORE LIKELY TO LEARN. AND THAT'S ACCELERATION.

students how amazing it feels to learn things. When we do, our students might just suspend their disbelief and engage with us on another level, opening the door for further acceleration.

4. **Create active, fast-paced learning experiences.** One of the norms with remediation is slowing down the learning and focusing on smaller and smaller aspects. Perhaps that's not always intended, but the trend in these types of efforts is to assume that students are far behind and need the pace to be slower so that they can learn. The opposite is true. Acceleration requires that we create active lessons in which students have multiple response opportunities. Remember, we're trying to build a memory trace through repetition and retrieval. The more often learners retrieve information, the more likely they are to remember it and be able to apply it. Some ideas for universal response for Roomies and Zoomies are provided in Figure 6.3.

> THE MORE OFTEN LEARNERS RETRIEVE INFORMATION, THE MORE LIKELY THEY ARE TO REMEMBER IT AND BE ABLE TO APPLY IT.

6.3 UNIVERSAL RESPONSE OPPORTUNITIES

Response Opportunity	Roomies	Zoomies
Response Cards	• Students hold up their personal whiteboards. • Students hold up index cards with *YES* on one side or *NO* on the other. • Students use a response fan with many options (true/false, A/B/C/D, thumb up/down). • Students submit responses through Google Forms and Microsoft Forms.	• Students hold up their personal whiteboards. • Students take a screenshot of their work and transfer it to the teacher. • Students hold up a CD case showing either red or green to indicate their response. • Students respond using reaction buttons (emoji checks). • Students submit virtual whiteboard responses. • Students submit responses through Google Forms and Microsoft Forms.
Polls	• Students respond to a Kahoot prompt. • Students complete an exit ticket in writing. • Students respond using Mentimeter. • Students add to a Jamboard.	• Students respond to a Kahoot prompt. • Students complete an exit poll on Zoom. • Students respond using Mentimeter. • Students add to a Jamboard.
Hand Signals	• Students hold up a number of fingers to indicate their level of agreement. • Students use American Sign Language to agree, disagree, ask a question, etc.	• Students hold up a number of fingers to indicate their level of agreement. • Students use the reaction buttons to indicate their response.
Chat	• Students respond in chat but do not hit send until a signal word has been given. • Students review the chat, copy another student's response that resonates with them, paste it into the chat, and explain why.	• Students respond in chat but do not hit send until a signal word has been given. • Students review the chat, copy another student's response that resonates with them, paste it into the chat, and explain why.

Note that we have just provided a few examples of the ways in which students can respond, retrieving information in the process. Each of these is also an opportunity for you to check for understanding and adjust the lesson accordingly. It's important to keep the pace brisk but not to the point that students experience excessive pressure. And it's important to remember the value of wait time; many of the response opportunities described above require thinking time. As a reminder, students need wait time to think and process. Students need to

➡ Listen to the question or prompt

➡ Process what they've heard

➡ Translate from another language, perhaps

➡ Build the courage to respond

➡ Indicate to the teacher that they are ready

Each of these takes time, and we must be careful not to privilege students who think fast, already know the information before we taught it, are fluent in the language of instruction, or have more power because of a demographic variable. Without sufficient wait time, combined with active and fast-paced lessons, we leave some students behind.

5. **Build students' confidence.** Confidence and competence are connected. But too often, we focus on students' competence and not their confidence to learn. We build students' confidence in a number of ways. First, we are trustworthy, and we provide honest growth-producing feedback. Thus, students come to understand that we have their best interests at heart and care deeply about their learning. In addition, we refrain from overcorrecting. We listen, noting errors and misconceptions that we can teach later, but we don't keep correcting students as it can compromise their confidence, which can lead to shutdown.

WHEN STUDENTS TELL US THAT THEY CAN'T DO SOMETHING, WE ADD YET.

When students tell us that they can't do something, we add *yet* and project the expectation that with additional learning, they will be able to accomplish great things. We're not suggesting that we falsely praise students or inflate their sense of current learning, but rather we recognize that learning is a journey and that errors are opportunities to learn. Remember, confidence is based on past experience, and educators can shape the current experiences that students have so that they tell a different story about themselves as they build the expectations they have for their own learning. Some advice for building students' confidence can be found in Figure 6.4.

6.4 WAYS TO BUILD STUDENT CONFIDENCE

Approach	Explanation
Set goals together.	One of the most effective ways of building student confidence is making sure everyone is on the same page about learning goals. Again, the value of clear learning intentions and success criteria cannot be overstated. To build confidence, students and teachers need to understand and agree upon the goals for learning.
Encourage self- and peer assessment.	Providing students the responsibility for helping both themselves and others improve learning by encouraging ownership of it is a huge step toward building student confidence. When students learn to self-assess, the role of the teacher becomes to validate and challenge rather than decide if students have learned. When we do this, student understanding, ownership, enthusiasm for learning, and, of course, confidence increase.
Give useful feedback.	Feedback should make someone feel good about where they are and get them excited about where they can go. This is the exact mindset that develops as we continue building our learners' confidence in the classroom.
Empty their heads.	Students tend to lose confidence in themselves because they feel they're struggling more than they are. Every once in a while, we've got to get learners to unpack everything in their heads through review and open discussion to show them just how much they've accomplished.
Show that effort is normal.	Nothing kills confidence more than for a student to think they're the only one in class that doesn't understand something. Focus on the effort that everyone is making. A good way of building student confidence in such a case is by having that struggling student pair up with one of the others who has aced the topic and get them to explain it.
Celebrate everyone's success.	Any kind of success in learning, no matter how big or small, deserves to be acknowledged and celebrated. This might mean more to some students than to others, but it's still a great way of building student confidence. After all, everyone is there in the classroom to learn together and to support each other on that path.

Source: Adapted from Wabisabi Learning. (n.d.). *6 ways of building student confidence through your practice*. Wabisabi Learning. wabisabilearning.com/blogs/mindfulness-wellbeing/building-student-confidence-6-ways

The final aspect of simultaneous learning that we explore is assessment. We present this last, yet we realize that assessment is important in each of the areas we have discussed thus far. We need assessments to know where to start learning, how to decide between synchronous and asynchronous learning, and to accelerate students' learning.

Conclusion

We have found ourselves in a different and unexpected situation in preK–12 teaching and learning. And to be very honest, none of us chose to be in a situation where some learners are physically in our classrooms, while others attend virtually and remotely. However, what we hope to have conveyed over the previous chapters is that we've got this! While the context is different, the principles behind clarity, planning, high-yield strategies and interventions, student learning, and assessment hold steady. Yet, our path forward is not simply the copying and pasting of what we did in face-to-face instruction into asynchronous learning and synchronous learning. We can't simply do what we have always done when we find ourselves teaching Roomies and Zoomies. While the principles of clarity, planning, high-yield strategies and interventions, student learning, and assessment hold steady, how we design and implement rigorous and engaging learning experiences requires us to make adaptations based on the local context. We filled the pages of this book with what to consider in making those adaptations. Teaching Roomies and Zoomies requires that we

WE'VE GOT THIS!

1. **Have clarity** about the most important learning outcomes for our students. This will help us decide what is best done asynchronously and what is best done with our Roomies and Zoomies.

2. **Capitalize on the potential of asynchronous learning** and use that valuable time to preview and review. Remember, we can use evidence from these tasks to help us decide where to go next in our teaching and our students' learning.

3. **Utilize synchronous learning** for collaborative learning and scaffolding of content, skills, and essential understandings. In doing so, we collect additional evidence of students' learning so that we can provide feedback that moves learning forward. Assessments are not a "gotcha," but "I've got you."

4. **Establish norms** for combining synchronous and face-to-face environments in simultaneous learning. We have to set up the environment for our Roomies and Zoomies to learn together.

5. **Develop learning experiences and tasks that maximize learner engagement** for all learners in all settings.

6. **Focus on acceleration and learning recovery**—stop deficit thinking! Our students are where they are, and there are specific things that we can do to ensure their learning.

References

Adesope, O. O., Trevisan, D. A., & Sundararajan, N. (2017). Rethinking the use of tests: A meta-analysis of practice testing. *Review of Educational Research, 87*(3), 659–701.

Almarode, J., Fisher, D., Thunder, K., & Frey, N. (2021). *The success criteria playbook. A hands-on guide to making learning visible and measurable.* Corwin.

Alter, P., & Haydon, T. (2017). Characteristics of effective classroom rules: A review of the literature. *Teacher Education & Special Education, 40*(2), 114–127.

Antonetti, J., & Garver, J. (2015). *17,000 classroom visits can't be wrong.* ASCD.

Bergmann, J., & Sams, A. (2012). *Flip your classroom: Reach every student in every class every day.* ASCD.

Berry, A. (2020). Disrupting to driving: Exploring upper primary teachers' perspectives on student engagement. *Teachers and Teaching.* Advance online publication. https://doi.org/10.1080/13540602.2020.1757421

Bill & Melinda Gates Foundation. (n.d.). *Literacy design collaborative.* http://k12education.gatesfoundation.org/blog/literacy-design-collaborative/

Buck Institute. (2021). *School Closures? Using PBL in remote learning.* https://www.pblworks.org/blog/school-closures-using-pbl-remote-learning

Cameron, C. E., Connor, C. M., & Morrison, F. J. (2005). Effects of teacher organization on classroom functioning. *Journal of School Psychology, 43*(1), 61–85.

Conroy, M. A., Sutherland, K. S., Snyder, A. L., & Marsh, S. (2008). Classwide interventions: Effective instruction makes a difference. *TEACHING Exceptional Children, 40*(6), 24–30.

Cruickshank, D. R. (1985). Applying research on teacher clarity. *Journal of Teacher Education, 36*(2), 44–48.

Cuban, L. (1993). *How teachers taught: Constancy and change in American classrooms, 1890–1990.* Teachers College Press.

Donker, A. S., de Boer, H., Kostons, D., Dignath van Ewijk, C. C., & van der Werf, M. P. C. (2014). Effectiveness of learning strategy instruction on academic performance: A meta-analysis. *Educational Research Review, 11,* 1–26.

Eccles, J. S. (2005). *Subjective task value and the Eccles et al. model of achievement-related choices.* In A. J. Elliot & C. S. Dweck (Eds.), *Handbook of competence and motivation* (pp. 105–121). Guilford Press.

Emmer, E. T., Evertson, C. M., & Anderson, L. M. (1980). Effective classroom management at the beginning of the school year. *The Elementary School Journal, 80*(5), 219–231.

Ericsson, K. A., Krampe, R. T., & Tesch-Römer, C. (1993). The role of deliberate practice in the acquisition of expert performance. *Psychological Review, 100*(3), 363–406.

Evertson, C. M., & Emmer, E. T. (1982). Preventive classroom management. In D. Duke (Ed.), *Helping teachers manage classrooms* (pp. 2–31). Alexandria, VA: ASCD.

Fendick, F. (1990). *The correlation between teacher clarity of communication and student achievement gain: A meta-analysis.* Unpublished doctoral dissertation, University of Florida, Gainesville.

Fisher, D., Frey, N., & Almarode, J. (2021). *Student learning communities. A springboard for academic and social-emotional development.* ASCD.

Fisher, D., Frey, N., Bustamante, V., & Hattie, J. (2020). *The assessment playbook for distance and blended learning: Measuring student learning in any setting.* Corwin.

Fisher, D., Frey, N., & Hattie, J. (2017). *Teaching literacy in the Visible Learning classroom, grades K–5.* Corwin.

Fisher, D., Frey, N., & Hattie, J. (2020). *The distance learning playbook, grades K–12: Teaching for engagement and impact in any setting.* Corwin.

Fisher, D., Frey, N., & Lapp, D. (2009). *In a reading state of mind: Brain research, teacher modeling, and comprehension instruction.* International Reading Association.

Fisher, D., Frey, F., Lapp, D., & Johnson, K. (2020). *On-your-feet guide: Jigsaw, grades 4–12.* Corwin.

Frey, N., Fisher, D., & Nelson, J. (2013). It's all about the talk. *Kappan, 94*(6), 8–13.

Kuhfeld, M., Soland, J., Tarasawa, B., Johnson, A., Ruzek, E., & Liu, J. (2020a). *Projecting the potential impacts of COVID-19 school closures on academic achievement* (EdWorkingPaper: 20-226). https://doi.org/10.26300/cdrv-yw05

Kuhfeld, M., Tarasawa, B., Johnson, A., Ruzek, E., & Lewis, K. (2020b). *Learning during COVID 19: Initial findings on students' reading and math achievement and growth.* https://www.nwea.org/content/uploads/2020/11/Collaborative-brief-Learning-during-COVID-19.NOV2020.pdf

Marzano, R. J. (2004). *Building background knowledge for academic achievement: Research on what works in schools.* ASCD.

MetLife. (2008). *The MetLife survey of the American teacher: The homework experience.* https://files.eric.ed.gov/fulltext/ED530021.pdf

Nuthall, G. (2007). *The hidden lives of learners.* NZCER Press.

Nystrand, M., Gamoran, A., & Carbonaro, W. (1998). *Towards an ecology of learning: The case of classroom discourse and its effects on writing in high school English and social studies* (No. 11001). National Research Center on English Learning & Achievement.

Palincsar, A. S., & Brown, A. L. (1984). Reciprocal teaching of comprehension-fostering and comprehension-monitoring activities. *Cognition and Instruction, 1*(2), 117–175.

Palmer, D., Dixon, J., & Archer, J. (2016). Using situational interest to enhance individual interest and science-related behaviours. *Research in Science Education, 47*, 731–753.

Rickards, F., Hattie, J., Reid, C. (2021). *The turning point for the teaching profession. Growing expertise and evaluative thinking.* Routledge.

Roediger, H. L., & Karpicke, J. D. (2006). The power of testing memory: Basic research and implications for educational practice. *Perspectives on Psychological Science, 1*, 181–210.

Rosenshine, B., & Berliner, D. C. (1978). Academic engaged time. *British Journal of Teacher Education, 4*, 3–16.

Rosenshine, B. V., & Furst, N. F. (1971). Research on teacher performance criteria. In B. O. Smith (Ed.), *Research in teacher education* (pp. 27–72). Prentice-Hall.

Saphier, J., Haley-Speca, M. A., & Gower, R. (2008). *The skillful teacher: Building your teaching skills* (6th ed.). Research for Better Teaching.

Simonds, C. J. (1997). Classroom understanding: An expanded notion of teacher clarity. *Communication Research Reports, 14*, 279–290.

Staarman, J. K. (2009). The joint negotiation of ground rules: Establishing a shared collaborative practice with new educational technology. *Language and Education, 23*(1), 79–95.

Visible Learning MetaX. (2021, January). https://www.visiblelearningmetax.com/

Wabisabi Learning. (n.d.). *6 ways of building student confidence through your practice.* Wabisabi Learning. wabisabilearning.com/blogs/mindfulness-wellbeing/building-student-confidence-6-ways

Wilfong, L. G. (2009). Textmasters: Bringing literature circles to textbook reading across the curriculum. *Journal of Adolescent & Adult Literacy, 53*(2), 164–171.

Wilfong, L. G. (2012). The science text for all. Using textmasters to help all students access written science content. *Science Scope, 35*(5), 56–63.

Index

About the Authors

Douglas Fisher, PhD, is professor and chair of Educational Leadership at San Diego State University and a leader at Health Sciences High and Middle College, having been an early intervention teacher and elementary school educator. He is the recipient of an International Reading Association William S. Grey citation of merit, an Exemplary Leader award from the Conference on English Leadership of the National Council of Teachers of English, as well as a Christa McAuliffe award for excellence in teacher education. He has published numerous articles on reading and literacy, differentiated instruction, and curriculum design, as well as books, such as *PLC+: Better Decisions* and *Greater Impact by Design, Building Equity,* and *The Distance Learning Playbook.*

Nancy Frey, PhD, is a professor in educational leadership at San Diego State University and a leader at Health Sciences High and Middle College. She has been a special education teacher, reading specialist, and administrator in public schools. Nancy has engaged in professional learning communities as a member and in designing schoolwide systems to improve teaching and learning for all students. She has published numerous books, including *The Teacher Clarity Playbook* and *The Distance Learning Playbook.*

(Continued)

John Almarode, PhD, is an associate professor of education and executive director of teaching and learning at James Madison University. He has worked with schools all over the world. John works alongside his colleagues in the College of Education with the Teacher Education, Teacher Induction, Teacher Leadership, and Educational Partnerships. John has authored multiple articles, reports, book chapters, and over a dozen books on teaching and learning.

Aleigha Henderson-Rosser, EdD, is a professor of educational leadership at Mercer University and executive director for instructional technology for Atlanta Public Schools. Her primary role as chief enthusiast and champion of innovative pedagogies and 21st century teaching and learning keeps her close to the work of instructional technology as a practitioner. She has served as a middle school science teacher, instructional technology specialist, coordinator of professional learning, and administrator for one of Georgia's first virtual high schools.

CORWIN
A SAGE Publishing Company

Helping educators make the greatest impact

CORWIN HAS ONE MISSION: to enhance education through intentional professional learning.

We build long-term relationships with our authors, educators, clients, and associations who partner with us to develop and continuously improve the best evidence-based practices that establish and support lifelong learning.

The PLC+ Books

Corwin's PLC+ framework is aimed at refreshing current collaborative structures and helps support teachers' decision making in the context of individual and collective efficacy, expectations, equity, and the activation of their own learning. The PLC+ books provide a foundation for this critical work.

PLC+

Better Decisions and Greater Impact by Design

What's this book about?

- Provides a brief history of PLCs
- Introduces the PLC+ framework questions and crosscutting themes
- Shows the PLC+ in action in various settings

When do I need this book?

- You want to understand the purpose of PLCs
- You want to learn a new framework for effective PLCs
- You want to reinvigorate and increase the impact of your existing PLC

The PLC+ Playbook

A Hands-On Guide to Collectively Improving Student Learning

What's this book about?

- Provides a practical, hands-on guide to implementing the full PLC+ cycle
- Guides PLC+ group members through 22 modules as they answer the five guiding questions and focus on the four crosscutting themes
- Offers modules comprising an array of tools that support implementation of the PLC+ framework

When do I need this book?

- You want to plan and implement the PLC+ framework in collaborative settings
- You want to implement the PLC+ model step by step in your own PLC

The PLC+ Activator's Guide

What's this book about?

- Provides guidance for the PLC+ team activators

When do I need this book?

- You are a PLC+ activator and want to do the best possible job for your group
- You are an activator and want to pre-plan the implementation of your PLC+
- You need help to guide the group in overcoming obstacles or having difficult conversations

Every student deserves a great teacher—
not by chance, but by design.

Read more from Fisher & Frey

Catapult teachers beyond learning intentions to define clearly what success looks like for every student. Designed to be used collaboratively in grade-level, subject area teams—or even on your own—the step-by-step playbook expands teacher understanding of how success criteria can be utilized to maximize student learning.

Disrupt the cycle of implicit bias and stereotype threat with 40 research-based, teacher-tested techniques; individual, classroom-based, and schoolwide actions; printables; and ready-to-go tools for planning and instruction.

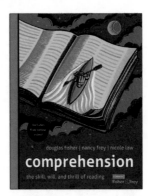

A new model of reading instruction that goes beyond teaching skills to fostering engagement and motivation. *Comprehension* is the structured framework you need to empower students to comprehend text and take action in the world.

When you increase your credibility with students, student motivation rises. And when you partner with other teachers to achieve this, students learn more. This playbook illuminates the connection between teacher credibility and collective efficacy and offers specific actions educators can take to improve both.

Tap your intuition, collaborate with your peers, and put the research-based strategies embedded in this roadmap to work in your classroom to implement or deepen a strong, successful balanced literacy program.

With cross-curricular examples, planning templates, professional learning questions, and a PLC guide, this is the most practical planner for designing and delivering highly effective instruction.

To order your copies, visit corwin.com/FisherandFrey